This is the BBC Home Service. Here is the news for today, May 17... the Air Ministry has just issued the following communique. In the early hours of this morning, a force of Lancasters of Bomber Command, led by Wing Commander G P Gibson DSO DFC, attacked with mines the dams of the Möhne and Sorpe reservoirs. These control two-thirds of the water storage capacity of the Ruhr Basin. Reconnaissance later established that the Möhne Dam had been breached over a length of 100 yards, and that the power station below had been swept away by the resulting floods. The Eder Dam, which controls the headwaters of the Weser and Fulda valleys, and operates several power stations, was also attacked and reported as breached. Photographs show the river below the dam in full flood. The attacks were pressed home at extremely low level with great determination and coolness in the face of fierce resistance. Eight of the Lancasters are missing.

B.B.C.
(LONDON)

The sun is still setting as three 617 Squadron Lancasters coast out from England heading for enemy territory on May 16, 1943, for Operation Chastise – the Dams Raid. (© Gary Eason / Flight Artworks)

DAMBUSTERS

Special thanks to the following for their
help and generosity in providing material
or images for this publication:

RAF Battle of Britain Memorial Flight
John Bell OBE DFC
Sarah James –
RAF Scampton Heritage Centre
Len Krenzler
The Lincolnshire Aviation Heritage Centre
Yvonne Masters
Mark Postlethwaite
Stuart Reid
Jim Shortland
Fred Sutherland
Robert Taylor
Phil Tetlow

Editor:
Clive Rowley MBE RAF (Retd)

Design:
Craig Lamb
Sarah Scrimshaw
Charlotte Turnbull

Reprographics:
Paul Fincham, Jonathan Schofield
Angie Sisestean

Picture research/admin:
Sarah Wilkinson

Publisher:
Steve O'Hara

Publishing director:
Dan Savage

Marketing manager:
Charlotte Park

Commercial director:
Nigel Hole

Published by:
Mortons Media Group Ltd,
Media Centre, Morton Way, Horncastle,
Lincolnshire LN9 6JR.
Tel: 01507 529529

Printed by:
William Gibbons and Sons,
Wolverhampton

ISBN:
978-1-911276-57-9

This edition © 2018
Mortons Media Group Ltd.
First published 2013.

Front cover
artwork by Phil
Tetlow (see page
110 for full story)

Welcome

from Squadron Leader Clive Rowley MBE RAF (Retd)

As the author of this special, commemorative publication, I feel that I should start by declaring my credentials which, on the face of it, have little do with being an expert on the Dambusters or the Avro Lancaster bomber. You see I am – or at least I was – a fighter pilot; I served for 36 years in that capacity with the Royal Air Force.

A background as a fighter pilot does not, though, rule out an interest in RAF Bomber Command's campaign during the Second World War. Indeed the precedent is set as the first author to write of the exploits of 617 Squadron, Paul Brickhill, was himself an ex-fighter pilot who flew Spitfires and Hurricanes during the war. His bestselling book – The Dam Busters – was first published in 1951.

I am proud to say that I, also, have flown many hours on Spitfires and Hurricanes with the RAF Battle of Britain Memorial Flight (RAF BBMF), finishing my full-time career as the officer commanding the RAF BBMF. As such, I was the temporary custodian of one of the finest collections of airworthy Second World War aircraft anywhere, including one of only two airworthy Lancasters in the world. On many occasions, some of them quite important, I have flown alongside the BBMF's mighty Lancaster in a Spitfire or a Hurricane, marvelled at the aura of the big bomber in the air – strangely shaped yet purposeful and somehow rather beautiful – and I have wondered what it was like for the men that flew them in far more dangerous circumstances. It has been my great privilege to meet many of those who did just that.

I share with every fighter pilot I have ever met, including those who fought in the Second World War, a deep respect for the men of Bomber Command and what they endured and achieved. Fighter pilots need to be brave, determined and aggressive, but the courage required by those who flew the heavy bombers during the war, is of a different order. They needed a steady, calm, unblinking, understated kind of courage and tenacity, sustained over long periods and night after night. Many were fearful men and rightly so, but they overcame their fear with sheer courage and appeared fearless, instilling confidence in those around them and particularly in the other members of their crew. Amazingly to us today, they did not think that what they were doing was anything particularly special. They were just doing the job they were given to do in wartime, to the best of their abilities... and they paid a heavy price.

I first read Paul Brickhill's book The Dam Busters when I was a boy and in many ways the story of the Dams Raid is like a Boy's Own story: Barnes Wallis and his madcap bouncing bomb, designed to be skipped to a target thus far considered invincible, by hand-picked airmen formed into a special squadron, who were, in some cases, little older than schoolboys.

In fact though, this single raid had an impact totally out of proportion to the small number of aircraft involved. It embodied the synergy of science and technology, weapons development and production, mission planning and practice, and the unflinching courage of the aircrews in the execution of a highly dangerous feat of arms.

Furthermore, it established a legend that still resonates today. The Dams Raid and the Battle of Britain are the RAF's most famous wartime exploits as far as most people are concerned. The story of the Dams Raid is a truly incredible one; a fabulous tale of ingenuity, daring and raw courage.

Seventy-five years on from Operation Chastise, as it was officially named, the Dams Raid still commands widespread attention. Crowds flock to commemorative events; documentaries continue to be made about it, and the 1955 box office-hit film The Dam Busters, starring Richard Todd as Guy Gibson and Michael Redgrave as Barnes Wallis, appears frequently on the television, deservedly so as it is a marvellous film. For most people in the 21st century, their understanding of what happened during the night of May 16/17, 1943, and the lengthy lead-up to the operation, is heavily influenced by that film; it is more about entertainment than education, and in 105 minutes much detail has to be left out and some facts are blurred or changed by artistic licence.

When I was asked if I would like to write this publication on the Dambusters and given a free rein over the content, it didn't take me long to decide that it was something I should do. It seems entirely

A BBMF flypast over Buckingham Palace to commemorate the 60th anniversary of the end of the Second World War. (Author Clive Rowley was flying the Spitfire on the Lancaster's left wing.) (Crown Copyright)

appropriate to me that in the year of the 70th anniversary of the Dams Raid, we should commemorate again the men of 617 Squadron and the engineering brilliance of Barnes Wallis and his colleagues at Vickers and Avro.

This is a fresh look at an old story with the benefit of some modern research to aid the process. The Dams Raid is an amazing story and one I thought I knew. It is a story of quality against quantity, demonstrating that exceptional ingenuity and skills can give a small force the effectiveness of one much larger. In researching and writing this publication I have realised that the achievement is even more extraordinary, even more daring and full of breathtaking courage than I had fully appreciated. I hope that I may have conveyed some of that. All military actions are made up of mistakes, myths and a few miracles – the Dams Raid contains them all – and I hope that I may have dispelled a few of those myths in these pages.

The Dams Raid would not have been possible without the men who made it happen. They were real people with human traits, personalities and flaws – more complex and more contradictory than has sometimes been portrayed. This is also a story of inspired leadership under conditions of almost unbelievable strain. I have attempted to give the reader some insight into what these men were really like. The dedication, fortitude, daring, skill, bravery and what today we call professionalism of the 19 seven-man crews that set out on this incredible feat of arms, 42% of whom did not return, makes for a story which should be retold for all time, so that they are not forgotten.

> *I have realised the achievement is even more extraordinary, even more daring and full of breathtaking courage than I had fully appreciated.*

For decades the results and effects of the Dams Raid have been downplayed or even condemned by a series of commentators, journalists and academics. In my opinion, and those of recent researchers, these views denigrate the sacrifice of those involved quite wrongly, especially those 53 who willingly gave their lives in the belief that they were making a difference. I hope that in this respect I have gone some way to setting the record straight.

I should point out that throughout this publication, for ease and for consistency, I have referred to the Upkeep bouncing bomb as a bomb, although it equally well fits the definition of a 'mine' or 'depth charge' and could be referred to as such. I should also mention, as it seems to be a controversial and emotive subject to some, that I have deliberately not used the name of Guy Gibson's famous dog, a ploy that will be obvious to those who hold strong views on this subject. While the name of the dog held no connotations, racist or otherwise, back in the 1940s, nor even when the Dam Busters film was released in 1955, today it is a word which can cause great offence. Some believe that not using the dog's name is political correctness gone mad, others are equally vociferous in recognising the offence it may cause in today's world. I am not in the business of changing history and would not dream of changing the name; I have simply opted not to use it in order not to cause offence.

For many the story of 617 Squadron starts and ends with the Dams Raid. This could not be further from the truth. Although 617 was originally formed to carry out one specific operation with a special weapon specifically designed for that purpose, it subsequently evolved into a specialist, precision bombing unit, able to target and to destroy specific military targets with pinpoint accuracy. The techniques developed by the squadron pointed the way towards the low-collateral-damage, precision bombing that is today expected by politicians and society at large. I have attempted to cover some of the brilliant post Dams Raid work done by the squadron in this publication.

By the end of the war 617 Squadron had, to quote Paul Brickhill: "Built up a record of individual and collective courage and skill which is unique. The story... cannot but make its readers feel humble in the face of such devotion, such self-sacrifice, and such courage." I cannot put it better and hope that readers will feel the same when they have read these pages.

Clive Rowley

Outbound

Artwork: Adam Tooby

The second 'three-ship' formation of specially-modified Lancasters of the 'First Wave' flying low over the North Sea en route to their targets.
    These aircraft, and the men flying them, were to play vital roles in the night's events. The lead aircraft, ED887 coded AJ-A, is flown by Squadron Leader 'Dinghy' Young DFC and Bar who later dropped the third and penultimate Upkeep against the Möhne dam, almost breaching it. He and his crew were all killed on the way home when they were shot down by German flak as they coasted out from Holland.
    The nearest aircraft is ED906 AJ-J flown by Flight Lieutenant Dave Maltby DFC; this was the aircraft and crew that subsequently breached the Möhne dam and one of the 11 that returned safely to base.
    The far aircraft is ED929 AJ-L, flown by Flight Lieutenant Dave Shannon DFC RAAF. This aircraft and crew dropped a successful Upkeep against the Eder, weakening it such that the next and final Upkeep breached the dam. They also made it home safely.

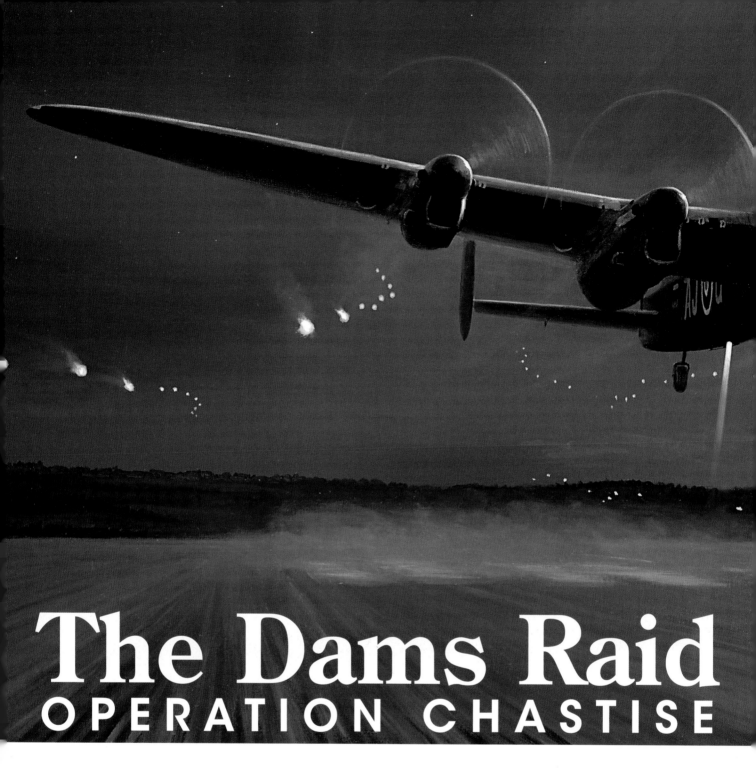

The Dams Raid
OPERATION CHASTISE

At 9.28pm local time, two minutes before sunset, on Sunday, May 16, 1943, a green Aldis lamp flashed from the runway control caravan on the airfield at RAF Scampton, situated just three miles north of Lincoln with its famous and ancient cathedral. The roar from the four Rolls-Royce Merlin engines of the Avro Lancaster bomber, which was lined up alongside, facing down the grass runway, rose to a crescendo. Then Lancaster ED927, coded AJ-E for 'Easy', thundered across the airfield, using most of the available length to haul itself into the sky with its heavy and peculiar load.

The undercarriage retracted and, as it disappeared at low level from the sight of onlookers, the flaps were raised and the engine note changed slightly as the propeller rpm was reduced. Royal Australian Air Force (RAAF) Flight Lieutenant 'Norm' Barlow

DFC, aged 32, had the honour of flying the first aircraft of 617 Squadron to set off on the special operation for which the unit had been formed – code-named Operation Chastise – which unknown to the men taking part at the time was to become legendary.

Barlow was one of those experienced pilots specially recruited by 617 Squadron for this mission and he had already completed a tour of 30 operations with 61 Squadron. Now, after six weeks of intensive training in low flying, he and his crew of six other airmen were glad to be getting on with it. The anxiety, stress, fear even, which nagged during the waiting stage was now replaced by a fatalistic attitude of 'what will be, will be'. They could concentrate and focus on the job in hand and even enjoy the thrill of action. They were not to know, but would not be surprised to have learned, that they would be dead before midnight.

Three more Lancasters followed Barlow's AJ-E at one minute intervals. AJ-W was flown by Flight Lieutenant Les Munro of the Royal New Zealand Air Force (RNZAF), AJ-K had the inexperienced 23-year-old Royal Canadian Air Force (RCAF) Pilot Officer Vernon Byers at the controls (he had only flown five previous operations), and AJ-H was flown by Pilot Officer Geoffrey Rice, another inexperienced operational pilot (these latter two pilots belie the widely held belief that all the pilots and crews who participated in the Dams Raid were experienced bomber 'aces'). Somewhat perversely, these first four Lancasters to take off were part of the designated 'second wave', which it was planned would follow a longer, more northerly, outbound route before attacking the Sorpe dam. The 'second wave' was actually intended to consist of five aircraft, but at this moment, Flight

'Dambusters - The Opening Shots'
(Gibson drops the first Upkeep at the Möhne)..
(© Mark Postlethwaite www.posart.com)

MARK POSTLETHWAITE GAvA '07

Lieutenant Joe McCarthy – a giant blond pilot from the USA, brought up in New York but serving with the RCAF, was frantically trying to get going in the mission's spare aircraft after his own, AJ-Q, 'Queenie', had developed an engine problem on start up. Far from considering this as a good excuse to stay behind as some might have done, Joe McCarthy had told his crew: "For Christ's sake, get into that spare aircraft before some other bugger gets there and we don't get to go." They were going to be late off.

It was still light as this initial wave of Lancasters took off and it would have been obvious to any observers on the ground, at the airfield or in the local area, that these aircraft looked different from standard 'Lancs'. These had a large chunk missing from their underbellies where the bomb bays had been cut away and they were each carrying a very large cylindrical-shaped

object which protruded below the aircraft. To reduce weight they also had their mid-upper/dorsal gun turrets removed.

At the airfield many of the 'expert' onlookers, who were used to 'normal' main-force bomber 'ops', may well have wondered what was going on, for they had been kept completely in the dark by the secrecy surrounding this operation and its purpose. Even the 617 Squadron crews themselves had not been told the targets – the dams – until earlier that day.

At 9.39pm three more of the specially-modified Lancasters took off together in formation; as the grass airfield allowed them to do when a narrower concrete runway would not. Leading this trio, in Lancaster ED932 coded AJ-G (which happened to be his father's initials), was the charismatic 24-year-old commanding officer of 617 Squadron, Wing Commander Guy Gibson

DSO and Bar, DFC and Bar. One of the most experienced pilots in Bomber Command, with 73 bomber 'ops' and 99 Beaufighter night-fighter sorties (with four night kills) to his credit, he was a man to lead from the front. Although his was the squadron's fifth aircraft to take off, he would be the first to enter Germany and the first to attack one of the dams with the operationally untested weapon they were carrying – the Barnes Wallis designed Upkeep 'bouncing bomb'. When he took-off, Gibson had already been awake and fully occupied with preparations for the night's operation for over 16 hours.

In formation with him as they thundered into the darkening sky was Lancaster ED909 AJ-P in the expert hands of the extrovert and charismatic 23-year-old Flight Lieutenant Harold 'Mick' Martin, an Australian with a full tour of 30 'ops' behind him and a DFC ribbon on his chest. On the other side of the

Above: The Upkeep from Barlow's AJ-E captured intact by the Germans. (Crown copyright)

Above right: Sergeant Jack Liddell – rear gunner in Barlow's AJ-E – aged 18 he was the youngest airman on the Dams Raid. (Author's Collection)

The aircraft crashed into the Waddenzee, with the deaths of all seven on board – the first fatalities of the operation.

formation was AJ-M flown by one of Gibson's closest and most trusted friends, 22-year-old Flight Lieutenant John 'Hoppy' Hopgood DFC and Bar. As they settled down into their three-ship loose 'vic' formation at very low level, heading south-east, the twilight was fading, presaging a clear, full moonlit night to come. After weeks of intensive training, practising flying the massive, 102ft wingspan bombers very low, first in daylight, then in simulated night conditions and finally at night and in formation, they were comfortable flying at heights of 60-100ft, sometimes even lower, in the dark and in formation.

As an ex-RAF 'modern' fighter pilot myself, I have many years of experience at low flying, mostly in fast jets, mostly at 250ft although sometimes lower, and generally considerably faster than the cruising speed of the Lancaster. With that experience I can categorically state that the grit, determination, courage and sheer skill to fly at the heights these Lancaster pilots did, in the dark, even in bright moonlight, simply cannot be overstated. That they attempted it at all, that they pressed on despite the dangers and difficulties and even enjoyed the thrill of it, is nothing short of amazing.

Two more 'vics' of three Lancasters took off from Scampton over the next 20 minutes until all nine aircraft of the 'first wave' were airborne and heading towards enemy territory at ultra-low level. The last of the nine to lift off was ED912 AJ-N flown by 22-year-old Australian Pilot Officer Les Knight. He and his crew were to have a major part to play later in the night and the story of their war, from the perspective of their front gunner, Sergeant Fred Sutherland, is told in detail elsewhere in this publication (see page 76).

It was almost dark as Joe McCarthy and his crew finally took off some 30 minutes behind schedule in the spare aircraft, ED825 AJ-T. This aircraft had been flown up to Scampton only that afternoon from Boscombe Down, where it had been used for weight and fuel tests; it was not in the best shape and it was not fitted with the special calibrated and converging

Aldis lamps that enabled the crew to fly accurately at 60ft by descending until the two spots of light converged into a figure eight.

About an hour and a half after their take-off, the first four aircraft of the second wave, bound for the Sorpe, were approaching the Dutch coast near the island of Vlieland which, according to the intelligence briefing, was supposed to be free of flak emplacements. Unfortunately this was not the case and as Les Munro crossed the coast in AJ-W at 60-70ft a line of tracer came up at them from the island and the aircraft was hit by a single, lucky 20mm anti-aircraft round. The intercom immediately went dead as the aircraft continued over the Zuider Zee and then circled while the crew assessed the damage. Fortunately there were no casualties aboard, but the master compass was demolished and the damage to the intercom was impossible to fix. Without the ability to communicate readily within the crew it was clear that the mission was impossible. Reluctantly and with some disappointment, Les decided that they had no choice but to abort their mission and return to base with their Upkeep bomb still aboard. They eventually landed safely back at Scampton, with the dubious honour of being the first aircraft back, at 36 minutes past midnight.

Others of the second wave fared even less well. Almost simultaneously with Munro's aircraft being engaged over Vlieland, Vernon Byers and his crew in AJ-K were crossing the coast over the heavily defended island of Texel having been blown south of their planned track by a stronger than forecast northerly wind over the North Sea. They were engaged by the anti-aircraft guns situated on the island. The aircraft was hit and set on fire; it crashed into the water near the Waddenzee, with the deaths of all seven on board – the first, but sadly by no means the last, fatalities of the operation.

Three minutes later as Geoff Rice approached the Dutch coast in AJ-H at extremely low altitude, knowing that this was essential for survival, he misjudged his height and hit the sea. The Upkeep bomb was ripped from the underside of the aircraft, the aircraft's tail wheel was rammed up into the rear fuselage, the hydraulic system was damaged and the rear gunner was drenched. Rice instinctively pulled the aircraft up and it staggered away from the water.

The crew had been the fortunate recipients of a miraculous escape from death, but they too had no choice but to abort the operation and return to base, eventually landing safely at 47 minutes after midnight.

Only 'Norm' Barlow and his crew in AJ-E for 'Easy' remained from the first four 'Second Wave' aircraft, but then at 11.50pm, shortly after crossing into Germany, AJ-E flew into high-voltage electricity cables. The Lancaster was engulfed in flames and crashed three miles east of Rees near Haldern with the loss of all seven men on board. Incredibly the Upkeep bomb on the aircraft rolled free without exploding in the crash and so the Germans were subsequently able to recover one of these new and highly-secret weapons intact for analysis. The rear gunner in Barlow's crew was Sergeant Jack Liddell who, at 18 years old, was the youngest airman to take part in the raid. He died before his adult life had properly begun. The wireless operator was 33-year-old Flying Officer Charles Williams DFC (RAAF), one of the older – although not the oldest – of those who flew on the raid. He had completed 30 'ops' with 61 Squadron before volunteering to join 'Norm' Barlow's crew on 617 Squadron. Only four hours before, Charlie had been writing a letter to his fiancée Gwen Parfitt, known as 'Bobby', a secretary in Nottingham, with whom he was deeply in love. He was looking forward to the leave he would get after the operation and the moment when they would be married later that week. 'Bobby' received Charlie's final letter on Tuesday, May 18, but as she was not his official next of kin, she received no telegram notification of his death. It would be some days before she found out that her fiancé was dead and their planned wedding and life together was not going to happen.

Now only Joe McCarthy's aircraft was left from the planned second wave; he and his crew had been late off but were gamely making up time and pressing on to their target – the Sorpe.

The nine aircraft of the first wave were faring better and they all coasted in without loss and pressed on through Holland and into Germany at very low level. They encountered some searchlights and flak, and 'Hoppy' Hopgood's aircraft AJ-M was hit when they were about 20 minutes away from the Möhne. The front gunner, Pilot Officer George Gregory DFM, was seriously injured or possibly killed, the

rear gunner, Pilot Officer Tony Burcher DFM, was slightly wounded by shell splinters in the stomach and lower leg, and Hopgood was hit in the face. The aircraft was also hit in the port wing, but despite the damage and injuries to his crew and himself, Hopgood decided to press on to the target.

As the first trio led by Gibson reached the Möhne, the last formation of the first wave, which was some 20 minutes behind, lost one of their aircraft when Flight Lieutenant Bill Astell DFC hit electricity cables, perhaps while trying to avoid anti-aircraft fire or as a result of being hit. His aircraft AJ-B was engulfed in flames, and exploded as it hit the ground near Marbeck, Germany, again with the loss of all seven crew members.

At almost exactly the same time Joe McCarthy in AJ-T reached the Sorpe after having had a little difficulty finding it due to mist forming in the valleys. He and his crew had done very well to make up lost time after their delayed take off. AJ-T had also encountered some flak from an armoured train on their way and, as they were to discover on landing later that night, shrapnel had burst their starboard tyre; otherwise they were in good shape.

Meanwhile, the five aircraft of the 'third (mobile reserve) wave' had begun taking off from Scampton at nine minutes past midnight. Six minutes later, all five were airborne. The last aircraft to take off of the total of 19 involved in the raid was ED924 AJ-Y flown by Flight Sergeant Cyril Anderson with his all-NCO crew. The aircraft headed south-east towards Germany, following the same route as the first wave, the roar of their Merlins gradually dying away until Scampton was shrouded in an eerie calm.

At the Möhne, Gibson circled the target and then made a dummy run over the dam to test the defences and "to look the place over". He and his crew were rather taken aback at the ferocity of the flak. There was a mixture of colours – different tracer for different types of shells – and because they were reflected on the calm water of the lake it gave the impression that there was twice as much as there

Above: This 1954 photo shows three of the Lancs from the Dam Busters film. The image is here because they are flying at the crucial 60ft. (Jan Kmiecik)

The aircraft was also hit in the port wing, but despite the damage and injuries, Hopgood decided to press on.

actually was. They thought that there were 12 guns firing at them from the towers of the dam and its surrounds; in fact there were six, but a single well-aimed or lucky 20mm shell from any of them would be enough to bring an aircraft down. The dam seemed huge and impregnable – it was, after all, 2550ft (777m) long, 121ft (37m) high and 26ft (8m) wide at the top; 102ft (31m) thick at the base – their Lancaster seemed tiny in comparison.

When the Lancaster's spotlights came on it gave the German defenders on the towers a clear target to aim at.

As the remainder of the first wave arrived and held off, awaiting their turn, they each orbited anticlockwise low over the hills some distance from the dam and away from the action.

At 12.28am Gibson made his attack run against the Möhne, coming in low over the surrounding hills and diving down towards the calm, black water of the lake. The twin spotlights, pointing out of the bottom of the

aircraft, were turned on and the navigator, Pilot Officer Torger Harlo 'Terry' Taerum (a Canadian of Norwegian extraction), started to control the height: "Down – down – down," talking the pilot down to 60ft above the water. Meanwhile the flight engineer, Sergeant John Pulford, was controlling the speed against the red mark on the air speed indicator at 232mph, using a small amount of flap to slow the aircraft and then increasing the power to hold it steady. When the Lancaster's spotlights came on it gave the German defenders on the towers of the dam a clear target to aim at and furious gunfire and tracers hurtled towards AJ-G, some bouncing off the water. In the front turret, the Canadian front gunner, Flight Sergeant George Deering, sprayed the dam's defences with 100% tracer rounds from his twin .303 Browning machine guns. Around 475 yards from the dam Pilot Officer Fred Spafford, the bomb aimer, released the Upkeep, which the wireless operator, Flight Lieutenant Bob Hutchison (RAAF), had ensured was spinning backwards at 500rpm. In the rear turret Flight Lieutenant Trevor Roper saw the bomb skip three times on the water as the Lancaster

hurtled over the dam and through the latticework of anti-aircraft gunfire. They had probably been helped by the element of surprise, as the German gunners had not expected an attack like this, and AJ-G escaped unscathed. Moments later a huge explosion sent a massive column of water some 1000ft into the sky, but when it settled the dam was still intact.

Next to attack, five minutes later when the disturbed water had settled down, was 'Hoppy' Hopgood in AJ-M. This time the German gunners on the dam knew what to expect – the element of surprise had gone – and they were ready. As AJ-M ran in towards the dam at 60ft it was hammered by gunfire. The aircraft was hit in both wings and in the nose and cockpit area, both port engines were hit, the inner port engine had to be feathered, the flight engineer was injured in the face, the wireless operator's right leg was shot away, the front gunner was probably killed and the navigator was possibly wounded or killed as well. One of the wing fuel tanks must have been hit because it ignited and flames leapt out, quickly engulfing most of the wing. In the confusion the Upkeep was released late and as the

burning Lancaster hurtled over the dam, trailing fire and smoke, the bomb skipped once and then bounced right over the wall, plummeting onto the power station below the dam. It exploded 90 seconds later with a vivid flash – the self-destruct fuse doing its job – sending a sheet of angry flame and debris into the air and destroying the power station. 'Hoppy' Hopgood struggled desperately to control his burning and crippled aircraft, trying to gain some height and to turn right to clear the ridge ahead to give his crew a chance of baling out, as he now ordered them to do.

When it had reached about 500ft there was a vivid flash, one wing fell off and the aircraft plunged into the ground three miles north-west of the dam. Miraculously, three of the crew had managed to get out; Flight Sergeant John Fraser DFM (RCAF), the bomb aimer, landed by parachute, unhurt; he was captured 10 days later having walked some 200 miles towards Holland and he spent the rest of the war as a POW. Pilot Officer Tony Burcher DFM (RAAF) also survived to become a POW, albeit with a badly injured back caused by striking the tail plane as he escaped from the disintegrating aircraft. Sadly, the seriously

Above: Wing Commander Guy Gibson leads the first three aircraft of the 'First Wave' low over Holland. (Picture © Gary Eason / Flight Artworks)

injured wireless operator, Sergeant John Minchin, did not survive the descent. Five of the crew of seven were killed. Before climbing into their aircraft at Scampton for the raid, 'Hoppy' Hopgood had confided in Dave Shannon that he did not think he would be coming back; his sense of foreboding, almost a premonition, had been proved correct, although he had not hesitated to do his duty.

Almost all the crews of the first wave saw AJ-M meet its fiery end and there was a long silence on the VHF radio – when before the airwaves had been full of chatter – as the crews absorbed the loss of their colleagues and the now all-too-obvious risks to their own survival. Two Upkeeps had been dropped without success, Hopgood's aircraft was burning fiercely in the distance and the enemy defences were fully alert. The German gunners had used each pause between attacks to replace overheated barrels, to rearm and prepare for the next attack, but now three of the six flak guns were out of action. The attackers did not know it, but their task had just become a little easier.

Gibson now ordered Mick Martin to attack and AJ-P for 'Popsie' began its run-in at 12.38am. This

time Gibson decided, with great courage, to fly alongside, slightly ahead, higher and to the right of Martin's aircraft, to distract the flak gunners, give them two targets to aim at to divide their fire and also allow his front gunner to engage the flak emplacements. This did not prevent Martin's plane from being hit but not seriously, and the bomb aimer, Flight Lieutenant Bob Hay DFC (RAAF) (the Squadron Bombing Leader), released the Upkeep, he thought, "dead on". However, the bomb sheered to the left, perhaps the aircraft had a small amount of bank on at release, but whatever the reason it hit the dam wall left of centre. As Martin pulled away, the Upkeep exploded sending another huge plume of water high into the air, but the dam remained intact.

Gibson now called up Squadron Leader Melvin 'Dinghy' Young DFC and Bar – the senior of his two Flight Commanders – in AJ-A for 'Apple' and told him to commence his attack. Gibson again flew to his right on the attack run, adding to the confusion by flashing his aircraft's lights on and off, and this time Martin flew to the left, giving the German gunners three targets and tripling the attackers' firepower against

the flak positions. When the Upkeep fell from Young's AJ-A it bounced three times, hit the wall and sank; it seemed the perfect strike, no deviation, dead centre and right up to the wall. A few moments later the bomb exploded in contact with the wall producing the, now familiar, great column of water. There was no immediate, apparent effect, to the disappointment of the crew and of those listening and waiting back in No. 5 Group HQ Ops Bunker at Grantham... but in fact the Möhne dam was beginning to crumble.

Meanwhile, 10 miles to the south-west at the Sorpe Dam, Joe McCarthy and his crew had been making dummy run after dummy run in their attempts to release their Upkeep on the correct parameters, against this entirely different target. The Möhne and Eder dams were arch gravity dams with thick bowed concrete and masonry walls designed to keep the water back by their weight, aided by their bowed shape. The Sorpe dam, on the other hand, was an entirely different structure consisting of a sloping earthwork embankment on both sides with a relatively thin concrete wall at its core. Barnes Wallis's Upkeep bomb was not really the right weapon to attack this

Above: 'First Strike' by Ivan Berryman. Wing Commander Guy Gibson in 'G-George' crosses the Möhne after dropping his Upkeep under a hail of anti-aircraft fire. (Reproduced by courtesy of Cranston Fine Arts)

Far left: A 'modern' photograph of the Sorpe dam from the attack direction, showing the different construction, the village of Langscheid bottom right and the wooded hills beyond the dam. (Author's Collection)

type of structure and it could not be used in the same way as at the Möhne and Eder. Wallis hoped that it might be possible to breach the Sorpe, but also expected that it would take at least five Upkeeps to do so. If all five aircraft of the second wave could drop their bombs in a concentrated spot against this undefended target, perhaps backed up by aircraft of the third wave, there was a chance of success. If they could blast the top off the dam, the water might do the rest. The crews were briefed to attack the Sorpe by flying along the length of the dam itself with the reservoir on their starboard side and with their port outer engine over the crest, dropping the Upkeep without it spinning or bouncing. The idea was that the bomb would roll down the water side of the dam before exploding underwater with the 'hydraulic' effect of the water to aid its destructive power.

At least the Sorpe was undefended, but Joe McCarthy and his crew had found it very difficult, nigh on impossible, to get down low enough and to achieve acceptable, let alone ideal, drop parameters due to obstacles and the terrain. At the western end of the dam was a tall church steeple in the village of

Langscheid, on a hill. They had to run in over the steeple, almost lifting a wing over it, to dive down to the dam and then, on the other side, there were steep wooded slopes which rose several hundred feet and which necessitated a steep climb away. They were hindered by not having the spotlights fitted to this spare aircraft, to allow them to judge their height more accurately over the dam. Joe McCarthy and his bomb aimer, Sergeant George 'Johnny' Johnson, were determined to get it right and on their first nine attempts one or the other of them was not satisfied and either McCarthy had pulled away or Johnson had called: "Dummy run". By 12.46am, the rest of the crew of 'T-Tommy' was beginning to lose patience with their skipper and bomb aimer as they flew round and round over enemy territory. Now, three minutes after 'Dinghy' Young had dropped the fourth Upkeep against the Möhne, they at last managed a good run and their Upkeep was released over the dam from only 30ft. When the bomb exploded, AJ-T was in a climbing turn to port to clear the wooded ridge ahead and the rear gunner, Flying Officer Dave Rodgers (RCAF), got a grandstand view of the tremendous

water spout, some of which actually hit the rear turret. For a moment he thought he was going to get drowned and exclaimed: "God almighty!" Orbiting the dam, the crew saw that there was some crumbling to the top but that was all.

Back at the Möhne, Flight Lieutenant Dave Maltby DFC in AJ-J for 'Johnnie' had been ordered to attack.

On the dam itself the German flak guns were now all out of action, although the Lancaster crews did not know this. The German soldiers had only rifles to fire at the attackers and the dam was almost defenceless. This time Gibson and Martin circled close to the dam to draw and suppress the remaining ground fire rather than flying alongside AJ-J as it ran in. At 45 minutes past midnight, a fifth Upkeep was released against the Möhne dam at exactly the correct height, speed and range, but even as the bomb fell away, the crew of AJ-J saw that the dam was crumbling. The Upkeep bounced four times, hit the dam wall, sank and when it exploded it sent up not only a column of water but also mud, stone and debris, rising high, silhouetted spectacularly against the moon. Then there was an excited yell on the R/T: "It's gone! It's

Above: 'Courage Beyond Fear' by Len Krenzler. Flight Lieutenant 'Hoppy' Hopgood's Lancaster ED925 AJ-M hurtles over the Möhne Dam on fire, its Upkeep bomb bouncing over the dam wall beneath it. (www.actionart.ca)

Far left: The Möhne Dam breached (German photo taken the morning after the raid). (Author's Collection)

OPERATION CHASTISE TIMELINE

21:28 AJ-E (Flt Lt Barlow) – first aircraft of Second Wave – takes off from Scampton.
21:29 AJ-W (Flt Lt Munro) takes off.
21:30 AJ-K (Plt Off Byers) takes off.
21:31 AJ-H (Plt Off Rice) takes off.
21:39 AJ-G, AJ-P and AJ-M (Wg Cdr Gibson, Flt Lt Martin and Flt Lt Hopgood) take off together (first of the First Wave).
21:47 AJ-A, AJ-J and AJ-L (Sqn Ldr Young, Flt Lt Maltby and Flt Lt Shannon) take off.
21:59 AJ-Z, AJ-B and AJ-N (Sqn Ldr Maudslay, Flt Lt Astell and Plt Off Knight) take off.
22:01 AJ-T (Flt Lt McCarthy) (last of the Second Wave) takes off 30 minutes late having switched to the spare aircraft.
22:56 AJ-W (Munro) crosses Dutch coast at Vlieland. Hit by flak one minute later.
22:57 AJ-K (Byers) hit by flak coasting in over Texel, Holland. (Seven dead.)
23:00 AJ-H (Rice) hits the sea near Vlieland. Upkeep ripped away – mission aborted, turns for home.
23:06 AJ-W (Munro) aborts mission due to flak damage and turns for home.
23:02 AJ-G, AJ-P and AJ-M (Gibson, Martin and Hopgood) cross the Dutch coast at the Scheldt estuary.
23:12 AJ-A, AJ-J and AJ-L (Young, Maltby and Shannon) cross Dutch coast.
23:13 AJ-T (McCarthy) crosses Dutch coast at Vlieland.
23:21 AJ-Z, AJ-B and AJ-N (Maudslay, Astell and Knight) cross Dutch coast.
23:50 AJ-E (Barlow) hits electricity cables and crashes near Haldern, Germany. (Seven dead.)
00:07 Gibson trio encounter flak. AJ-M (Hopgood) hit but continues.

00:09 AJ-C (Plt Off Ottley) – first of the Third (Reserve) Wave – takes off.
00:09 AJ-S (Plt Off Burpee) takes off.
00:12 AJ-F (Flt Sgt Brown) takes off.
00:14 AJ-O (Flt Sgt Townsend) takes off.
00:15 AJ-Y (Flt Sgt Anderson) takes off – last aircraft of 19.
00:15 AJ-B (Astell) hits electricity cables and crashes near Marbeck, Germany. (Seven dead)
00:15 Gibson's trio reach the Möhne.
00:15 McCarthy reaches the Sorpe, having made good time.
00:26 Young's trio reach the Möhne.
00:28 Gibson attacks Möhne. Good bomb – no apparent effect.
00:33 Hopgood attacks Möhne. Hit by flak. Bomb bounces over the dam and destroys the power station beyond. AJ-M crashes. (Five dead; 2 POW.)
00:36 AJ-W (Munro) lands at Scampton with its Upkeep bomb.
00:38 Martin attacks Möhne. Bomb hit dam left of centre with no apparent effect.
00:43 Young attacks Möhne. Good bomb – no initial effect, but dam actually seriously damaged and beginning to crumble.
00:46 McCarthy attacks Sorpe after nine 'dummy' runs. Good bomb – no apparent effect.
00:47 AJ-H (Rice) lands at Scampton.
00:49 Maltby attacks Möhne. Good bomb – Möhne dam breached.
01:30 Gibson first to arrive at Eder, followed by Shannon, Maudslay and Knight.
01:39 Shannon attacks Eder on his sixth attempt. Good bomb – no apparent effect.
01:45 Maudslay attacks Eder. Bomb hits

dam parapet and explodes underneath AJ-Z, which limps away damaged.
01:52 Knight attacks Eder on his second attempt – good bomb, Eder dam breached.
01:53 AJ-S (Burpee) (Third Wave ingress) crashes due to the pilot being blinded by a searchlight over Gilze-Rijen airfield, Holland. (Seven dead.)
02:35 AJ-C (Ottley) (Third Wave ingress) shot down by flak north-east of Hamm. (Six dead, one POW.)
02:36 AJ-Z (Maudslay) shot down by flak over Emmerich near the Dutch border on the way home. (Seven dead)
02:58 AJ-A (Young) shot down by flak coasting out near Castricum aan Zee, Holland, crashed just off the coast. (Seven dead.)
03:10 AJ-Y (Anderson) aborts the mission and turns for home when the crew became hopelessly lost after taking evasive action.
03:14 AJ-F (Brown) attacks the Sorpe after six 'dummy' runs. Good bomb but only minor damage and dam held.
03:11 AJ-J (Maltby) lands at Scampton.
03:19 AJ-P (Martin) lands at Scampton.
03:25 AJ-T (McCarthy) lands at Scampton.
03:37 AJ-O (Townsend) drops bomb at the Ennepe without effect.
04:06 AJ-L (Shannon) lands at Scampton.
04:15 AJ-G (Gibson) lands at Scampton.
04:20 AJ-N (Knight) lands at Scampton.
05:30 AJ-Y (Anderson) lands at Scampton still carrying its Upkeep bomb.
05:33 AJ-F (Brown) lands at Scampton.
06:15 AJ-O (Townsend) lands at Scampton – the last of 11 aircraft out of the original 19 to return.

gone!" Gibson went in for a closer look and saw clearly the water pouring out through the vast breach in the centre of the dam. Millions of cubic metres of water were now gushing down the valley like a tsunami; the spray creating a fog that shrouded the deluge. On the VHF radio there were all sorts of excited shouting and chatter, over-excited delirium from normally calm professionals, until Gibson told them to be quiet. The night's work was only half done, they had yet to tackle the Eder, but their first and primary objective had most emphatically been achieved. The remains of 'Hoppy' Hopgood's aircraft still burned a few miles away, a dull red glow on the ground. 'Hoppy' had been avenged.

Gibson ordered Maltby and Martin to set off home and then led the remaining three aircraft of the first wave that still had bombs on board, and 'Dinghy' Young who was now the deputy leader, to the Eder some 25 miles away to the south-east. Due to the misty conditions they had some trouble finding the Eder among the hilly terrain. Gibson located it first and fired a red Very flare over the dam to give the others the position. The Eder was undefended, not least because the Germans considered that the terrain surrounding it made it impossible to attack from the air. It certainly posed the greatest challenge and risk from a flying point of view. The only feasible attack direction required a dive from 1000ft down a valley to the lake leaving the prominent Waldeck Castle on its knoll to port, levelling off over the water pointing towards a spot on the spit ahead of the dam, then banking hard to turn sharp left, rolling out and levelling off with only some seven seconds left before

crossing the dam. This was difficult enough in any circumstances, but in a heavy Lancaster made even less manoeuvrable by the weight of the Upkeep bomb, which weighed over 9000lb, and the gyroscopic effects of the bomb spinning underneath which resisted changes of direction, and in the dark, it was almost asking the impossible. Beyond the dam were further hazards with a ridge of hills ahead, only one third of a mile further on, the tops of which were some 500ft above the dam.

At 1.30pm 20-year-old Flight Lieutenant Dave Shannon DFC (RAAF) in AJ-L for 'Leather', had the first of three failed attempts to get it right. Gibson then gave him a rest and sent in Squadron Leader Henry Maudslay DFC in AJ-Z for 'Zebra'. He too could not achieve the release parameters for an Upkeep drop with two dummy runs. Shannon was called in again and on their sixth attempt the crew of 'L-Leather' released their bomb; it bounced twice, hit the dam and exploded, but as the water settled, the wall was still intact. Now Maudslay tried again and at 1.45am the crew of AJ-Z released their Upkeep. A moment after 'Z-Zebra' hurtled over the dam wall with full emergency power set on all four engines to climb over the high ground ahead there was a blinding flash as the Upkeep, having bounced only once, hit the parapet and exploded almost underneath the aircraft. Gibson quickly called

Above: Joe McCarthy's crew, from left: Sergeant G Johnson, Pilot Officer D A MacLean, Sergeant R Batson, Flight Lieutenant J C McCarthy, Sergeant W G Ratcliffe, Sergeant L Eaton. Flying Officer D Rodger not in the picture.
(© IWM TR1128)

The Eder was undefended... the Germans considered the terrain made it impossible to attack.

Opposite page: The Eder Dam breached (photo taken the morning after the raid). (Author's Collection)

on the radio asking 'Z-Zebra' if they were okay. There was a faint reply: "I think so – stand by", and that was all, as AJ-Z limped away towards home. When the smoke from the explosion cleared from the valley the dam was still standing solid.

That left only 22-year-old Pilot Officer Les Knight and his crew in AJ-N – the last aircraft, the last bomb, the last chance. Les Knight and his crew also needed a dummy run against this most difficult target. All sorts of advice was being proffered over the R/T by the other aircraft, so much so, in fact, that it was a distraction and Les ordered that the VHF radio be turned off in their aircraft. On their second run they got it exactly right, perfectly lined up, at the right speed and at 60ft, they released the Upkeep 450 yards from the dam at 1.52am. The bomb bounced three times, hit the wall and sank. As AJ-N was screaming to clear the hills beyond, the Upkeep exploded, a huge column of water rose into the sky and the dam began to collapse. Just like the Möhne, the water was spewing out through the breach, rushing down the valley and flooding everything in its path. As the crews watched the breach was getting larger as the water washed the sides away. It was an extraordinary scene and a truly awesome sight.

Just as the crews at the Eder were enjoying their success, the third wave aircraft were over Holland still making their way eastwards towards the targets. One minute after the Eder was breached, 25-year-old Pilot Officer Lewis Burpee DFM (RCAF) and his crew in AJ-S strayed too close to the German night fighter airfield at Gilze-Rijen at ultra-low level. The anti-aircraft guns did not have time to react but a searchlight on a tower between the command post and a hangar swung into action and illuminated the Lancaster, which was flying so low the searchlight beam was almost horizontal. This presumably blinded the pilot, as the aircraft tore through some trees and then crashed into the ground and caught fire in the motor transport yard on the edge of the airfield. Seconds later its bomb exploded, creating a huge shockwave and killing all seven on board. Lewis Burpee's English wife was expecting their first child. The explosion destroyed the HQ of NJG/2, the German night fighter unit, which was based at Gilze-Rijen. The German searchlight crew claimed a rare searchlight 'kill'.

Around 30 minutes later, AJ-C, another aircraft of the third wave, was continuing eastwards over Germany when it was coned by searchlights and then

Seconds later its bomb exploded, killing all seven on board. Lewis Burpee's wife was expecting their first child.

shot down by flak north-east of Hamm at 2.35am. Pilot Officer Warner 'Bill' Ottley DFC (RCAF) and five others of his crew were killed. Miraculously, the rear gunner, Sergeant Fred Tees, who had swapped places with the front gunner at the last minute, was thrown clear in the crash and survived, although severely burned and with shell splinters in his back, to spend the rest of the war as a POW.

Meanwhile Henry Maudslay and his crew in AJ-Z had almost reached the Dutch border on their way home. Perhaps the aircraft was damaged or some of the crew were wounded, because the aircraft had strayed south of the planned return route and it flew directly over the heavily defended oil storage facilities at Emmerich am Rhein. One minute after Ottley and AJ-C were sent crashing in flames, 'Z-Zebra' was engaged by the flak guns defending Emmerich and shot down in flames to crash in a field to the north of the town at 2.36am. Another seven men of the squadron died here.

Some 20 minutes later at 2.58am, 'Dinghy' Young and his crew in AJ-A were approaching the sandy beaches near Castricum aan Zee within spitting distance of the open sea on their way home. He was probably flying extremely low, but even so 'A-Apple' was hit by flak as they coasted out; it plunged into the sea and onto a sand bar just off the coast with the

loss of all seven on board. This was to be the last aircraft lost that fateful night, eight of the 19 aircraft sent out on the raid did not return and 53 of the Squadron's aircrew had been killed.

Three of the five aircraft of the third wave were still trying to make it to their targets, but at 10 minutes past three in the morning Flight Sergeant Cyril Anderson and his crew in AJ-Y aborted the mission and turned for home. They had become hopelessly lost after veering well off track as a result of taking various evasive actions to avoid flak and searchlights. The GEE radio navigation signals were being jammed effectively by the Germans, mist was shrouding landmarks, the rear turret was playing up and dawn was beckoning. They eventually landed back at Scampton at 5.30am with the Upkeep still on board.

There were now only two aircraft of the five from the third wave still active: AJ-F and AJ-O.

In 'F-Freddie' Flight Sergeant Ken Brown (RCAF) and his all NCO crew had been directed to the Sorpe. Despite the mist, they found the Sorpe without too much difficulty, but then experienced the same sort of problems as Joe McCarthy and his crew in trying to get down onto the dam for a successful bomb drop. At least they had the spotlights to help them assess their height and they also hit on the idea of dropping flares to illuminate the dam and surrounding area and to help them to keep their bearings as they repositioned between dummy runs. After nine dummy runs they released their Upkeep accurately on the 10th run over the dam. The same massive explosion and plume of water that other crews had experienced ensued, but although they

thought they might have done some damage to the crest of the dam it remained intact. They had done what they had been asked to do and set off home, eventually landing safely at 5.33am.

For some reason the final crew, that of Flight Sergeant Bill Townsend in AJ-O, had been directed to the Ennepe Dam rather than the Sorpe. They had a harrowing flight to the target avoiding flak, but thought that they had found the Ennepe despite the mist and, after two dummy runs, they dropped the last Upkeep of the night, which unfortunately bounced twice and then sank short of the dam, exploding without any effect upon it (modern research suggests that Townsend may have attacked the Bever dam seven miles south of the Ennepe, not that it really matters). The return journey for Bill Townsend was an epic piece of low flying as dawn broke behind them, making them a very visible target to the German flak gunners. They came under particularly heavy fire, like many others had done, as they coasted out between the Dutch islands of Texel and Vlieland flying extremely low. The aircraft was hit, but not fatally, and thanks to Bill Townsend's superb low flying they escaped and were astonished to see the Germans actually skipping shells off the sea towards them as they raced for safety. Over the North Sea one of the engines developed an oil pressure problem and had to be shut down, so they returned on three engines at a slower speed. Landing back at Scampton at 6.15am, the battered Lancaster was the last one down out of the 11 that returned, almost all damaged to varying degrees.

Operation Chastise was over. Its like would never be seen again.

Above: Pilot Officer Burpee's crew on 106 Sqn. From left: Warrant Officer Joe Brady (rear gunner), Sgt Bill Long (front gunner), Sgt Guy Pegler (flight engineer), Pilot Officer Lewis Burpee (pilot). The two on the right, Flt Sgt Eddie Leavsley and Sgt George Gooding, did not join 617 Sqn with the rest of the crew. (www.ww2images.com)

Möhne breached

Artwork: Adam Tooby

Lancaster Type 464 ED906 AJ-J flown by Flight Lieutenant Dave Maltby DFC hurtles over the Möhne dam as its Upkeep bomb explodes against the dam wall behind it.

The previous Upkeep, dropped by Squadron Leader 'Dingy' Young DFC and Bar, had weakened the dam wall and started it crumbling. This, the fourth Upkeep dropped against the Möhne, breached the dam. By this time the German flak had lessened and both the AAA guns on the towers of the dam had fallen silent.

Maltby and his crew survived the Dams Raid only to be killed four months later on an aborted 617 Squadron

Dams Raid
Photographic reconnaissance

Above: Spitfire PR Mk.XI EN654 photographed in 1943. These specially modified Spitfires, painted in their PR blue camouflage, were fitted with long focal length cameras in the rear fuselage; they carried extra fuel in the wings in place of the guns and so were unarmed. The deeper nose fairing accommodated a larger oil tank for long-range missions. This type of aircraft conducted the pre- and post-attack reconnaissance for the Dams Raid.

Right: One of the most famous aerial photographs of the war. Jerry Fray's recce photo from 30,000ft on the morning after the Dams Raid, showing the breach in the Möhne dam. (Crown Copyright)

In 1943, Flying Officer Frank G 'Jerry' Fray (later Squadron Leader Fray DFC) was a Spitfire photographic reconnaissance (PR) pilot with 542 Squadron flying out of the RAF's principle PR base at Benson, in Oxfordshire. Jerry had joined the RAF in 1940 and commenced his flying training in the summer of 1941 at Hullavington, Wiltshire. After completing his training and qualifying on Spitfires, he volunteered for photographic reconnaissance duties and was posted to Benson in 1942. Jerry flew his first PR 'op' to Den Helder in July 1942.

On May 15, 1943, he was tasked to conduct the final, highly-secret reconnaissance of the Ruhr Dams, before the attack on them by the specially modified Lancasters of 617 Squadron with their 'bouncing bombs'. This was Jerry's 36th operation and he photographed the targets from 30,000ft in his Spitfire PR XI to provide the 617 Squadron crews with the latest information on their targets for their briefing for the Dams Raid.

On the morning of May 17, at 7.25am – only about an hour after the last 617 Squadron Lancaster had landed from the Dams Raid – Jerry Fray took off from Benson in Spitfire PR XI EN343, alone and unarmed as always, to conduct a post-attack reconnaissance of the Möhne, Eder and Sorpe Dams. His was to be the first 'recce' aircraft over the targets after the raid. The targets were some 300 miles from Benson and when he was still 100 miles from the Ruhr he could see what looked like a bank of cloud to the east. As he got closer he

A beautiful picture of a beautiful aircraft: Spitfire PR XI EN654 undergoing an air test in the hands of the legendary Spitfire test pilot Jeffrey Quill in 1943. Photo reconnaissance Spitfires of this type produced detailed images of the dams to help with the planning of Operation Chastise and, after the raid, gathered information so that the results could be assessed. (© IWM E MOS 1325)

Above: A remarkable wartime image of Spitfire PR XI EN343 – the aircraft flown by Jerry Fray to conduct the recce of the dams after the raid. (© IWM CH18430)

Right: *The Daily Telegraph* of May 18, 1943, with the photograph of the breached Möhne dam on its front page.

realised it was, in fact, the sun glinting on floodwaters that had filled the valley below the Möhne Dam.

From 30,000ft he surveyed the scene of devastation below. He later admitted that he felt overcome by the immensity of the scale of destruction. After taking his photographs of the Möhne, he moved on to the Eder valley, where the destruction was even greater. More than three quarters of the water in the dam had escaped and it was still rushing out through the breach. Jerry had just finished his second run over the Eder when he spotted two enemy fighter aircraft approaching. He immediately turned for home at full throttle to ensure that the valuable intelligence information he had gathered was not lost. He landed back at Benson three hours and 35 minutes after take-off to be met by the station commander eager for his verbal report and his photographs.

Two more PR sorties were flown from Benson that day to complete the coverage of the Eder and Sorpe Dams. The photographs that were produced were pin sharp and showed that the both the Möhne and Eder dams had been breached but the Sorpe remained intact.

In stark contrast to the secrecy that normally surrounded PR operations, the Air Ministry released Jerry Fray's photograph of the breached Möhne dam to the press. The image appeared on the front pages of the newspapers with triumphant reports of the

success of the Dams Raid. It became one of the most famous aerial photographs of the Second World War. At the time, of course, the identity of the photographer and that of hundreds like him who regularly braved the enemy's skies in their specially adapted sky-blue camouflaged Spitfires, without escort or armament, was kept secret. Jerry Fray was awarded the DFC in December 1943.

The Results

DISASTER FOR GERMANY... OR BRITISH FAILURE?

A German photo of the
Möhne taken the morning
after the raid.'
(Author's Collection)

Above: Air Chief Marshal Sir Arthur Harris, Commander-in-Chief of Bomber Command. (Crown Copyright)

Above right: Aftermath of the flooding at Neheim. (Author's Collection)

Excluding the three aircraft that returned early having aborted their missions, precisely half of the remaining 16 Lancasters on the Dams Raid were lost, along with the 56 airmen aboard (42% of those who took off for the raid), although three of those miraculously survived and saw out the war as POWs. Compared with the typical loss rates on Bomber Command 'main force' raids at this time, which ran at 4-5%, this was a very heavy percentage loss rate indeed. It is inevitable that questions have been asked, at the time and ever since, as to whether it was worth it.

The Dams Raid was indisputably an enormous propaganda triumph, not least because the British jumped at the chance to make it so. At a stroke it raised the morale of the RAF's Bomber Command and the British public, and helped in convincing Americans that the war was going well. The news of the Dams Raid was trumpeted on the radio and in newspapers, along with the Axis surrender in North Africa a few days before, and the free world was suddenly being given a positive glut of good news stories and war successes. Prime Minister Winston Churchill was in Washington at the time and when he addressed Congress on May 19, 1943, he was able to use the Dams Raid to make his point on the importance and successes of the strategic bombing campaign.

Congress erupted into cheers. It was a perfectly timed riposte to those in the United States who had been critical of British bombing efforts. The propaganda value of the raid was not limited to the free world either, as news of it was dropped by leaflets to the occupied countries. On the other side, in Berlin, reaction to the attack was one of barely contained shock and horror. What made this attack so troubling was the apparently small numbers of aircraft used and the fact that the weapons, of awesome power, had been delivered with such precision. The Möhne and Eder dams were iconic structures in Germany, a source of national pride, symbols of German mastery

Harris was almost placing the raid on a par with the pointlessly courageous Charge of the Light Brigade.

and power; their breaching was a huge affront to German prestige and self-esteem.

However, beyond the obvious propaganda value, the issue of whether the Dams Raid actually caused any serious damage to the German war effort, especially when balanced against the cost, has long been a source of controversy. Bearing in mind that the gaps in both breached dams had been filled by October 1943 and no decisive damage had been done to the Sorpe, was the operation really worthwhile?

After the event, one of the most powerful British critics of the raid was, perhaps surprisingly, none other than the irascible Commander-in-Chief of Bomber Command, Air Chief Marshal Sir Arthur Harris. He had fought tooth and nail to prevent the raid happening in the first place, believing it to be an attempt to attack a so-called 'panacea' target, and he had fiercely resisted the concept of elite units, which 617 Squadron obviously was. When ordered by the Chief of the Air Staff to facilitate the formation of the special squadron and the plans for the raid he had supported it as any good military man would do.

For a while, immediately after the attack, he had gone along with the euphoria that its success had brought. Subsequently and privately though, he continued to view the raid as an indulgence. In a telling letter to the Assistant Chief of Air Staff, Air Vice Marshal Norman Bottomley, he wrote: "…I have seen nothing… to show that the effort was worthwhile except as a spectacular operation." Towards the end of the war he wrote to the Chief of Air Staff, Sir Charles Portal, saying: "It achieved nothing compared with the effort and the loss. Nothing that is, but a supreme display of skill, gallantry, devotion and technical ingenuity." He was almost placing the raid on a par with the pointlessly courageous Charge of the Light Brigade some 90 years earlier. It is perhaps not surprising that the views of such an eminent and authoritative expert on Bomber Command operations have been accepted by many ever since.

Since the war, a series of commentators, journalists and academics have variously condemned the results of the Dams Raid as having little effect on the German war effort and therefore not being worth the losses suffered by 617 Squadron. Their writings contain phrases such as: "…virtually devoid of any military significance", "… misdirected courage",

"… scant effect on German war production". These critics have pointed towards the rapid restoration of the dams and have suggested that the long term impacts of the raid were marginal. In my opinion, these views denigrate the sacrifice of those involved quite wrongly.

The bare facts of the immediate results of the Dams Raid make it clear that it was a great technical success and achieved two of its principal aims. If the Sorpe could have been breached as well the effects would have been far greater and wider reaching, but the construction of this dam proved virtually invulnerable to attack, two Upkeeps were certainly not enough to breach it and we will never know whether five would have done. Even when the dam was bombed by 9 Squadron with 12,000lb Tallboy 'earthquake' bombs in October 1944, taking several direct hits, it stood firm.

Below the Möhne and Eder though, the immediate effects of the tsunami-like flooding were truly catastrophic for all those unfortunate enough to be in its path. At the Möhne a gap 250ft (76m) broad and 72ft (22m) deep had been blasted through the dam between the two towers. The anti-torpedo nets had been dragged through the breach by the force of the water and left stranded on the other side. Below the dam wall the 20 ton turbine from the power station, which was totally destroyed, was carried more than 100m downstream. Of the 132 million cubic metres of water in the reservoir, 116 escaped in the first 12 hours. In the flood, buildings up to a distance of 41 miles (65km) from the dam were destroyed, as were bridges 31 miles (50km) away. The 'tidal' wave reached Neheim, eight miles (12.9km) from the dam where the Möhne and Ruhr rivers met, about 15 minutes after the dam was breached and as the floodwaters flowed through the town they were 30ft high. A factory producing naval mines at Neheim was totally destroyed, as was the camp housing the foreign female forced labourers, 479 of whom were killed. At the narrowest point of the Möhne valley floodwaters reached a height of 50ft.

Within six hours the floodwaters had reached the junction of the Ruhr and the Rhine rivers 93 miles (148.5km) distant. Along the length of the Ruhr many pumping stations were affected and, ironically, many towns were left without water supplies (including Hamm, Hagen, Bochum and Dortmund). One of the most important stations of the Rhine-Westphalia

Power Supply Company, the pump storage plant and power station at Herdecke, was flooded to a depth of 2m. It was subsequently out of action for weeks. Final official figures for the Möhne and Ruhr valleys showed one power station destroyed, two flooded and others affected; 12 war production factories were destroyed and many more damaged (sources vary between 91 and 114); 25 road or rail bridges were destroyed and 21 railway bridges damaged (eight of them severely); numerous pumping stations, and water and gas supply facilities were also affected; 96 buildings had been completely destroyed and a further 872 were damaged.

Nearly 3000 acres of farmland were ruined. Below the Möhne there were 1294 deaths, officially reported as 476 German dead with 69 missing, and 593 foreign dead with 156 missing. The flood waters also disrupted river and canal transport, which was vital to the Germans; after the floods subsided, canal banks had to be repaired and long stretches of the rivers and canals had to be dredged of silt.

Above and below: The morning after at the Möhne Dam. (Author's Collection)

Within six hours the floodwaters had reached the junction of the Ruhr and the Rhine rivers 93 miles distant. Ironically, many towns were left without water.

Above and below: The Möhne on the morning following the Operation Chastise raid. (Author's Collection)

At the Eder, a breach 230ft (70m) wide and 72ft (22m) deep had been caused, and 30,000 tons of masonry was torn from the structure. Of the 202 million cubic metres of water in the reservoir, 154 million escaped. Four power stations were put out of action. Only 47 people died below the Eder, but large swathes of arable farmland were washed away and the harvest for that year completely ruined. Fritzlar airfield was partially flooded. As with the Möhne, the 'tidal wave' destroyed and damaged railways, locomotives and rolling stock in its path.

While the breaching of the dams was undoubtedly a disaster for Germany in the short term, the long term effects as the flood waters subsided have proved more difficult for historians to assess. Recent research using German documentation gives a different picture to the one touted for many years by critics of the raid. In the immediate aftermath the failure in the water supplies to the industrial towns meant that incendiary bombs could not be extinguished and when Bomber Command attacked Dortmund on the night of May 23, with 826 aircraft, 2000 buildings were destroyed.

Much of the flooded land below the Möhne and Eder was covered in silt and could not be tilled for years afterwards.

Four nights later Essen was hit, again with similarly devastating results. The effects on the Ruhr were not all short term though. For example the waterworks at Fröndenberg and Echthausen, which were important for regional coalfields, were totally

out of action for four months. Only a 'tolerable' level of water supplies was restored to the towns via the severely damaged waterworks supplying Neheim-Hüsten, Soest and Herdecke. The loss of farmland, agricultural products and cattle in the floods also had serious long-term implications; much of the flooded land below the Möhne and Eder was covered in silt and could not be tilled for years afterwards. In Germany in June 1943, the month after the raid, meat rations for 'normal customers' were reduced for the second time in two months.

Meanwhile the effects on German industry were not as insignificant as some believe. Steel production in the Ruhr fell by 20,000 tons in the second quarter of 1943, partly because of the lack of water for the cooling process. Coal extraction fell radically for several weeks after the raid – this essential commodity was needed both at power stations and for the steel industry – it dropped by 813,278 tons in May alone, almost half of which could be attributed to the Dams Raid. Albert Speer, the German minister for armament and war production, later said that though a breach in the Sorpe would have represented "a complete disaster", the Dams Raid was nevertheless a "disaster for us for a number of months". In his book Inside the Third Reich, Speer said: "A torrent of water had flooded the Ruhr Valley. That had the seemingly insignificant but grave consequence that the electrical installations at the pumping stations were soaked and muddied, so that industry was brought to a standstill, and the water supply to the population imperilled. That night, employing just a few bombers, the British came close to a success which would have been greater than anything that they had achieved hitherto with a commitment of thousands of bombers."

The problems created for the Germans caused by the smashing of the dams were threefold. Firstly there was the material damage that has been described, factories, power stations, bridges, railways, buildings and, of course, the dams themselves needed to be repaired or rebuilt. It has been estimated that the cost of the rebuilding was a staggering £5.9 billion in today's money. Secondly there was the water shortage. Water was needed as a power source, in the extraction of coal and for steel production, as well as for drinking and sanitation, and for use by the fire services.

This water shortage was short term and not critical as there were reserve supplies such as underground sources, but it did mean that the dams

needed to be rebuilt quickly before the autumn and winter rains or there would be a long-term problem the next year.

Which leads to the third consequence, if the dams were to be rebuilt in the time required it would take massive amounts of manpower to do so. The rapid reconstruction of the dams required 7000 Organisation Todt (OT) labourers to be drafted away from building the Atlantic Wall, which as a direct result was incomplete when D-Day and the Allied invasion of Normandy occurred the following year. The breach in the Möhne dam was closed on September 23, 1943, and that in the Eder soon after, but when Generalfeldmarschall Rommel reached France in December 1943, to take over the defences, he was horrified at what he discovered. There were barely any defences at all, let alone any kind of 'wall'. One of the reasons for this was that earlier in the summer of that year, when the OT should have been building bunkers, gun positions, anti-tank ditches and beach defences, large numbers of its workers had been transferred to Germany to rebuild the dams.

RAF Bomber Command's Battle of the Ruhr officially lasted from March to the end of July 1943; it cost some 1000 aircraft that did not return and 7000 men. The average percentage losses suffered during the Battle of the Ruhr were about 4% overall; those for Operation Chastise (42%) were far higher. However, when the losses on the Dams Raid in real terms (eight aircraft and 56 men) and the vast amount of damage caused are compared to the entire Battle of the Ruhr, it doesn't seem such a bad balance sheet.

It is time to put the record straight, not least for the sake of those involved and especially for those 53 who willingly gave their lives in the belief that they were making a difference. The Dams Raid was not just a spectacular propaganda triumph; it also struck a devastating blow against the heart of the Third Reich and seriously dented the Germans' ability to wage war. The amazing technical ingenuity and the skill and courage of the airmen of 617 Squadron were not in vain. The cost to the Germans of repairing the damage wrought by the Dams Raid was enormous – psychologically, materially, logistically and financially – it was one that they simply could not afford. The effects of the raid had ramifications that made the D-Day invasion less costly to the Allies. This was not, as many have said, a military failure and the achievements of the extraordinary Dams Raid should never be belittled.

Above: RAF reconnaissance photo of the Eder valley showing infrastructure damage. (Crown Copyright)

The raid was not just a propaganda triumph; it also struck a devastating blow against the heart of the Third Reich.

Barnes Wallis

THE ENGINEER, SCIENTIST AND INVENTOR

Anyone with knowledge of the Dams Raid knows that it would not have taken place without the genius, ingenuity and persistence of the aeronautical engineer, scientist and inventor Dr Barnes Wallis (later Sir Barnes Wallis CBE FRS RDI FRAeS). Most people's impressions of Barnes Wallis are based on the brilliant portrayal of him by Michael Redgrave in the famous 1955 film The Dam Busters, which is quite an accurate depiction in some respects.

But who was Wallis... and what was he really like?

Barnes Wallis was born at Ripley, Derbyshire in 1887; the second of four children. His father was a doctor who set up a practice in the East End of London, but as he suffered from polio, working was difficult and money was always tight. Barnes was obviously academically able and he was given the opportunity to take a competitive entrance exam for a foundation scholarship to Christ's Hospital, near Horsham in Sussex, a public school founded in 1552. Barnes came seventh out of 110 boys who took the scholarship exam and received a place at the school. He proved to be a natural at mathematics, English and science and by the end of his school education he had decided that he wanted to be an engineer.

He left school at 17 and secured his first job in January 1905, working at the Thames Engineering Works at Blackheath in south-east London, building ship engines. In 1908 Wallis gained an apprenticeship with J Samuel White's shipbuilders, based at Cowes on the Isle of Wight, to train as a marine engineer, gradually working his way up in the profession. He left White's in 1913 when an opportunity arose for him to join Vickers Limited (Aviation Department) as one of the designers in the firm's airship development programme.

Barnes Wallis with a model of a deep
penetration bomb of his own design.
(© IWM HU 92134)

Below: A Type 464 (Provisioning) Lancaster dropping a practice Upkeep at Reculver in May 1943, a few days before the Dams Raid. (© IWM FLM 2365)

Shortly after the outbreak of the First World War, Wallis found himself unemployed when the Admiralty decided to cut back on airship spending. He decided to join the services but this plan was scuppered when he failed the eyesight test. He overcame this disappointment by applying again and when he was asked to strip before his medical examination, he made sure that he did so near the sight testing card, and quickly memorised it. For a while Wallis was a sub-lieutenant in the Royal Naval Air Service working on airships at Walney Island. However, soon after he had joined up, the airship designing team was recalled and the War Office was persuaded to release Wallis back to the team. He worked on the design of airships for some years, but by 1922 Vickers had moved on to other projects and Wallis was made redundant again. He decided to take a degree in engineering via the University of London External Programme and he also became a teacher at a young gentlemen's academy in Switzerland.

It was in 1922 that Wallis met Molly Bloxam, a cousin-in-law, at a family tea party. She was only 17 and in her last year at school; he was 35 and did not at the time appear to have good prospects, so her father forbade them from courting. However, he allowed Wallis to write to Molly with the aim of helping her with her maths. They ended up writing hundreds of letters to each other, enlivening them with fictional characters. The letters gradually became personal, romance blossomed and Wallis proposed to her on her 20th birthday. They married in April 1925. Their age difference never seemed to matter and they remained happily married until his death. By the time of their wedding Wallis was back at Vickers and was now the assistant chief designer, working on a renewed airship programme, including the giant

R100, the largest airship ever built at the time. The era of the airship was almost over though, and Wallis was moved to Vickers Aviation at Weybridge, Surrey, in 1930.

It was then that the couple bought White Hill House, a large family house in Effingham, Surrey, where they lived for 49 years until his death. Cautious with money and never extravagant, as a result of the experiences of his earlier life, this was a major commitment for Wallis, but one that paid dividends for him and his large family. The couple had four children of their own and also adopted Molly's sister's two children after they had been orphaned when their parents were killed in an air raid, so for many years the house and garden were full of the sound of children. It was a classic Surrey house of period design with mock Tudor beams, set back from the road and looking out onto a golf course; it was a quiet haven for Wallis, away from the politics and the stress of his war work. He was a good father to the children; warm and loving, although strict too, and he would spend time playing with them when he could. In his spare time Wallis would play golf and he also enjoyed wood carving (at which he was quite accomplished), listening to music on the gramophone and reading. He was a regular church-goer – he served on the local parish church council – and he was also a church bell ringer. He was essentially a peace-loving man, which seems a strange thing to say about a man who designed some of the most awesome weapons of the Second World War, but although he was a devout Christian he was also a strong patriot.

By January 1943, Wallis was 54 years old and he looked every bit the absent minded professor, although actually nothing could have been further from the truth. His hair was thick and white and

somewhat untamed, he often wore spectacles and his suits – more country than city – were cut for practicality rather than tailored to fit his big frame. He had a gentle, modest nature and an affable manner which could be quite disarming, but which hid an inner steeliness, determination and not a little stubbornness. He was both highly organised and pragmatic; he was something of a perfectionist, a brilliant mathematician and draughtsman, who could remember figures and technical particulars and recall them with extraordinary detail. He had been involved in the design of the Vickers Wellesley and he invented the geodetic structure used in the Wellington bomber. He may have been slightly eccentric but he was now respected as one of the foremost aeronautical engineers and designers in Britain.

Norman Boorer, a draughtsman who worked alongside Barnes Wallis at Vickers, said of him at this time: "He was a good engineer who insisted on quality work. He reckoned he could do anything he wanted to do if he gave enough thought to it, provided he did not upset any basic laws of physics. He did not let problems stand in his way. It was difficult working with him. You had to have a tremendous amount of patience. He could be a very cheerful, pleasant and thoughtful man at certain times, but at other times he could be very awkward."

There is a popular theory that Barnes Wallis was the only person to realise the potential damage that would result if the great dams of Germany were destroyed. Those who have seen the famous film based on the raid will remember how Wallis dreamt up the idea and then put into practice, but this is not factually correct and he cannot be credited with the original idea. From as early as October 1937, Air Ministry staff had been drawing up plans for implementation in the event of war with Germany. Among these, Plan WA5 highlighted the need to attack Germany's war industry in the Ruhr, and from these studies emerged the idea that attacking the Möhne and Sorpe dams would cause widespread flooding which would help to achieve the aims.

This style of thinking chimed with Wallis who believed that modern warfare depended on industrial production which, in turn, relied on sources of power. He concluded that the best way to attack the enemy was to disrupt the war effort – rather than concentrating on tactical battles – destroying the enemy's ability to fight at source. While production facilities could be dispersed and difficult to target, Wallis reasoned that coal mines, oil fields and dams made static targets of great importance, if the right weapons could be designed to attack such large structures effectively.

From the beginning of the war onwards, aside from his paid job as assistant chief designer for Vickers, Wallis spent time and brain power on the problem of how to attack the dams. It became something of a personal campaign and fortunately he had a great many useful contacts in the corridors of power and in the scientific research world who aided his efforts. Despite numerous disappointments and knock-backs, Wallis was not to be put off. By July 1942 experiments and research had proved that if a bomb of a size that could be carried by the Lancaster bomber could be detonated underwater, in contact with the dam wall, it would breach it. The only problem was how to achieve that, and it is here that Barnes Wallis's amazing ingenuity and sheer genius

came to the fore with his idea for the 'bouncing bomb', which he had been working on for some time.

He had originally tested the concept with a catapult and his daughter Elizabeth's marbles, firing them at a low angle onto some water in a tub on the patio of the house at Effingham, to make them skip across the surface. Subsequently, formal trials at the National Physical Laboratory's water tanks had shown that if the bomb was given backward spin before release, this increased the distance it travelled before first impact with the water, it struck the water at a lower glancing angle and it increased the distance that it travelled while ricocheting. This spin also had the beneficial effect of making the bomb or mine stick to the dam wall as it sank after it had hit it, so that when detonated at a pre-determined depth it would still be in contact.

Perhaps not surprisingly, Wallis was having difficulty persuading the RAF and in particular Bomber Command to pursue his idea. It must have seemed incredibly far-fetched, even after he was able to show a film of successful trial drops carried out in January 1943 from a Wellington at Chesil Beach, to prove that it actually worked. The chief disbeliever was the Commander-in-Chief of Bomber Command, Air Chief Marshal Sir Arthur Harris, who decreed it: "Tripe of the wildest description... not the smallest chance of it working." He also wrote: "The war will be over before it works and it never will." Nonetheless, Wallis continued to lobby for his weapon and in early February 1943, he gained support from Churchill's scientific adviser, Professor Lindemann, previously not just sceptical but actively hostile to the plan. Despite his protests that "the weapon is barmy", Harris was overruled by the Chief of Air Staff, Air Chief Marshal Sir Charles Portal, who gave the plan his backing, though guardedly at first.

When the green light was given to go ahead, Wallis had not even produced any detailed drawings for the weapon, no trials of the full-size weapon had

He had tested the concept with a catapult and his daughter's marbles, firing them at a low angle in a tub

Above: Sir Barnes Wallis in later life with a Lancaster behind him. (© PA Images)

Above right: Wartime picture of Barnes Wallis (© PA Images)

been done and there were only eight weeks left before it would be too late to attack the dams that year, as the water levels would begin to fall. Wallis later confessed that when he left the conference at which the plan had been given the go-ahead he felt physically sick "because somebody had actually called my bluff".

There were numerous other technical difficulties to overcome during the brief period in the rush to the Dams Raid, not least the problem of the original bomb design's spherical wooden casing shattering on impact with the water when dropped from an aircraft. This led eventually to the outer casing being deleted, leaving the Upkeep as a cylindrical shaped weapon. In addition, trials showed that it would be necessary to drop the weapon from much lower than had originally been thought; the Lancaster crews would have to drop Upkeep from only 60ft. That the project was completed in time, allowing the raid to go ahead as planned on the night of May 16-17, 1943, is a testament to the brilliance of Barnes Wallis in all his capacities and capabilities – as an engineer, designer and scientist.

To him it was shattering to think so many young men, some of whom he had met the night before the raid, were now dead.

After the Dams Raid, when the losses among the 617 Squadron crews became apparent, Barnes Wallis was distraught and inconsolable. He found the realisation that eight crews had not returned very hard to come to terms with. For so long he had been concentrating purely on destroying the dams and designing the weapon to do that, he had not really considered the likely human cost involved. To him it was shattering to think that so many young men, some of whom he had met personally on the night before the raid, including Hopgood, Maudslay and Young, were now dead. It was something that lived with him for the rest of his life. Sir Arthur Harris sent a telegram to Barnes Wallis after the raid which read: "We in Bomber Command owe everything to your knowledge, skill and persistence in the face of discouragement and disappointment for the outstanding success achieved." Later Wallis was

presented with a large photograph of the breached Möhne dam, which Gibson and others signed and which proudly hung on his office wall for the rest of his working life.

Barnes Wallis went on to design the remarkable 12,000lb (six ton) Tallboy 'earthquake', bunker-busting bomb used by IX and 617 Squadrons, and its big brother the 22,000lb (11 ton) Grandslam dropped only by 617 Squadron's specifically modified Lancaster B1 Specials. These remarkable weapons were designed for attacks against special targets where deep penetration was required and were very much ahead of their time.

During the war, after the Vickers factory at Brooklands was badly bombed in September 1940, the design office had been dispersed to the nearby Burhill Golf Club in Hersham. Wallis returned to Brooklands in November 1945 as head of the Vickers-Armstrong research and development department, based in the former motor circuit's 1907 cubhouse. Here he and his staff worked on many futuristic aerospace projects, including supersonic flight and 'swing-wing' technology (later used in Tornado and other aircraft types). By 1948, a massive 19,533sq ft Stratosphere Chamber (which was the world's largest facility of its type and still survives at Brooklands Museum) was designed and built beside the clubhouse and became the focus for much R&D work under Wallis's direction in the 1950s and 1960s. Wallis also invented the non-misting, glassless mirror. One of these unbreakable mirrors made from non-flammable polyester was even sold to Buckingham Palace. Wallis never really stopped designing and inventing. In fact, he carried on working until he was forced to retire at the age of 83, and even this did not stop him.

Barnes Wallis was awarded £10,000 for his war work by the Royal Commission on Awards to Inventors. Such were his feelings of sadness at the loss of so many airmen on the Dams Raid that Wallis donated the entire sum to his old school Christ's Hospital to allow it to set up the RAF Foundationer's Trust, which allows the children of RAF personnel killed or injured in action to attend the school. In 1968 he received a knighthood for his work and service to his country. He died on October 30, 1979 aged 92.

The Weapon
UPKEEP – THE 'BOUNCING BOMB'

The operational version of Barnes Wallis's amazing 'bouncing bomb' – code-named Upkeep – was a cylindrical-shaped device 5ft (1.53m) long and 51in (1.3m) in diameter, which weighed 9250lb (4195kg). Wallis had originally intended that the bomb would be spherical with flattened ends, and the initial trial weapons contained the steel cylinder within a spherical cover of pine staves held together with steel straps, making it look like a fat beer barrel.

Wallis believed that the spherical shape would help to minimise aerodynamic drag during carriage and was essential to ensure the maximum skipping distance; it was also more likely to bounce in a straight line without veering off to one side, being more forgiving than the cylindrical shape if the aircraft was not exactly wings level at release. During the early test drops it was found that the straps failed on first impact with the water, causing the outer wooden casing to shatter. Strengthening the straps did nothing to stop the failures. However, on some drops, as the outer case shattered, the central cylindrical core broke free and bounced on by itself, eventually proving that the spherical wooden casing should be deleted from the design.

The cylindrical version of the weapon also had the advantage that it was easier to load onto the aircraft, as it fitted underneath the Lancaster, which the spherical version would not have done as it would have been too large.

The construction of Upkeep was relatively simple, which was just as well, because when the decision was made in Whitehall on February 26, 1943, to go ahead with the Dams Raid there were only 80 days

left until the ideal date to attack the dams when the reservoirs would be full and water levels at their highest. Astonishingly, Wallis's team actually completed the drawings for the subsequent manufacture of the weapon in less than 36 hours. Upkeep consisted of two circular end plates of ⅜in steel, bolted with 32 bolts to a cylinder formed of ½in sheet steel. Two 'L-section' rings, 20in in diameter, were bolted to the end plates to allow the weapon to be supported and spun on the aircraft. These rings were joined by six tie rods, which passed right through the cylinder from end to end to provide rigidity. The Upkeep cylinders were manufactured at the Vickers works at Barrow-in-Furness and at Elwick and Walker on Tyneside.

Above: The Upkeep from Barlow's aircraft was captured intact after the Lancaster was shot down over Germany. A nervous looking official stands by the bomb, giving it scale.
(© IWM HU 62922)

Below: Upkeep in the Imperial War Museum at Duxford.
(Author's Collection)

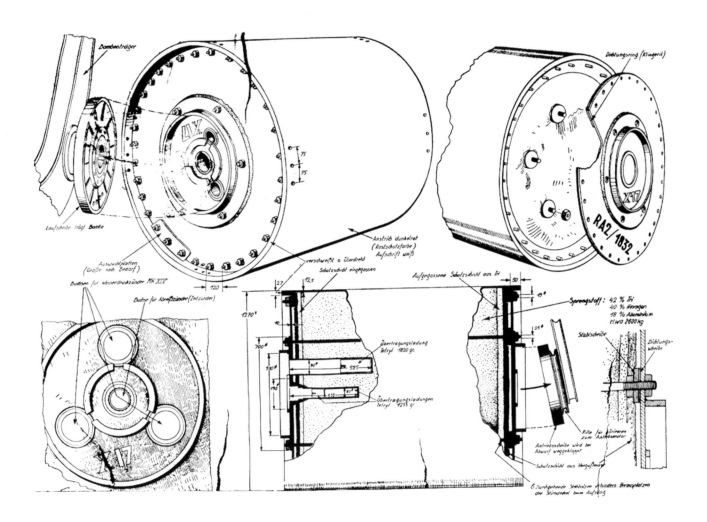

The bombs were filled with 6600lb of Torpex high explosive (HE) at the Royal Ordnance Factory at Chorley in Lancashire. Torpex was a comparatively new explosive at the time, intended primarily for use in torpedoes. Throughout this publication, for ease and for consistency, the Upkeep is referred to as a 'bomb', but it equally well fits the definition of a mine or even depth charge and could be referred to as such. This is clear from the types of fuses fitted to it, which were designed to detonate the bomb underwater at a specific depth. Three hydrostatic pistols (there were three to give some redundancy) of the type used by the Navy in depth charges (Mk.XIV pistols) were fitted in one of the end plates, arranged 120° apart in a circle around the rotational axis. These were set to detonate the bomb at about 30ft underwater.

If an Upkeep was dropped on land the hydrostatic pistol would not fire and, given the highly secret nature of the weapon, it was decided to fit a self-destruct fuse with a 90 second delay, in a firing pocket, on the rotational axis of the weapon. If dropped in the 'armed' state, a Bowden cable would be pulled out on release, to initiate the detonator of the self-destruct fuse. In the case of the Upkeep which the Germans captured intact from Barlow's aircraft after it was shot down en route, it is likely that the bomb was ripped from the aircraft with its retaining calliper arms still attached, so that the cable was not pulled out and it was, therefore, not destroyed. In all the other cases of aircraft being shot down or crashing, including Hopgood's bomb that landed on the power station below the Möhne dam, the 90 second delay self-destruct fuse did its job.

Upkeep was spun backwards (in the opposite direction to an aircraft wheel rotating) at 500rpm before its release. This backspin gave some added stability during its fall, but the main advantage was the generation of a certain amount of aerodynamic lift caused by the interaction of the spin with the forward motion, which prolonged the bomb's flight time before first impact and reduced the impact angle, which helped it to skip or 'bounce'. Another useful effect of the backspin was to keep the weapon in contact with the dam wall as it sank. Spinning a 9000lb mass at 500rpm underneath an aircraft and then releasing it cleanly was always going to be problematic.

The weapons needed to be balanced, just like the wheels of a car, or there would be significant vibration transmitted to the aircraft. Each Upkeep was carefully and individually balanced on a special rig during manufacture and preparation, by adding small metal balance weights to the end plates to minimise vibration. This was done both prior to loading the explosive and again afterwards. Even so, the Dams Raid crews reported various levels of juddering through their aircraft, "like driving on a cobbled road", was one comment; it was no doubt dependent on how well their particular bomb had been balanced.

The first drawings for the manufacture of the full-scale Upkeep were completed on February 28 and the first live drop of a full-scale, production standard, inert Upkeep from a Lancaster took place at Reculver, off the north Kent coast, on April 13, 1943. The specially-modified Lancaster was flown by Squadron Leader 'Shorty' Longbottom, a RAF test pilot attached

The Dams Raid crews reported various levels of juddering through their aircraft, "like driving on a cobbled road".

Above: An inert Upkeep bounces ashore close to observers during drop trials at Reculver in April 1943.
(© IWM FLM 2343)

to Vickers-Armstrong. The early trials were largely unsuccessful, the spherical wooden cases shattering on impact with the water and even when the decision was made to use just the bare steel cylinder, some bombs either shattered or just sank. Wallis realised that the drop height needed to be reduced and the final drop parameters became 232mph at 60ft. This was asking much of the pilots, and Wallis also explained to Wing Commander Guy Gibson, OC 617 Squadron, how critical the release range was too: "If you undershoot nothing will happen, if you overshoot the mine will go over the top of the dam… or the mine might hit the parapet and explode underneath your tail." Dropped accurately, at an ideal range of 475 yards from the dam, the bomb was expected to explode about 100 yards behind the aircraft. "You'll be okay," Wallis told Gibson. "There's not much blast from an underwater explosion; besides the parapet will protect you."

> *"You'll be okay," Wallis told Gibson. "There's not much blast from an underwater explosion."*

The first successful drops of two cylindrical-shaped inert Upkeeps did not occur until April 29, only two and a half weeks before the planned date for the raid. On May 11, 12 and 13, some of the 617 Squadron crews were each able to test drop an inert Upkeep at Reculver. On May 13, 'Shorty' Longbottom dropped a live Upkeep out at sea away from prying eyes. It skipped seven times, travelling about 800 yards, sank and then exploded spectacularly, causing a column of water about 1000ft high to rise into the sky. None of the Dams Raid crews had themselves dropped a live Upkeep before the raid itself and many had not even dropped an inert version.

No original plans of the operational Upkeep are known to have survived (the best surviving contemporary plans available today are those produced by the Germans from analysis of Barlow's bomb). The colour which the Upkeeps were painted has long been a topic of interest to modellers and artists, but the actual colours of all the Upkeeps used on the raid is not recorded. In line with standard RAF practice, the inert, practice Upkeeps should have been painted grey and the HE-filled ones green. However, Henry 'Doc' Watson, the 617 Squadron Armament Officer, stated in an interview before his death that the Upkeeps for the Dams Raid were delivered to Scampton painted in red primer paint. Some of those used on the raid are believed to have been painted black to blend in with the lower fuselages of the Lancaster aircraft, but German details of the captured example refer to a "dark red" colour, so it is probable that at least the Upkeep on Barlow's aircraft was in primer red and there may have been others the same colour taken on the raid.

Only somewhere slightly over 50 live Upkeeps were ever built; 17 were expended on the Dams Raid. After the raid the remarkable Barnes Wallis 'bouncing bomb' was never again used 'in anger'. The remaining Upkeeps that had not been used were disposed of in 1946 after the war had ended. The technical details of the 'bouncing bomb' were kept secret and not declassified until 1963.

The Aircraft
LANCASTER TYPE 464 (PROVISIONING)

O peration Chastise – the Dams Raid – would not have been possible without the remarkable four-engine heavy bomber, the Avro Lancaster, the only aircraft, at the time, capable of carrying the Upkeep weapon and with the performance, range and manoeuvrability required to complete the operation successfully.

The Lancaster's participation in the legendary Dams Raid gave it a place deep in the British public's psyche and ensured its iconic status.

THE AVRO LANCASTER

Designed by Avro's chief designer, Roy Chadwick, as an evolution of the troublesome Manchester, the prototype Lancaster was built at Chadderton and took to the air for its maiden flight on January 9, 1941, from Manchester's Ringway Airport. The first flight of a production-standard Lancaster took place on October 31, 1941. 44 Squadron at Waddington became the first RAF unit to receive the new aircraft for operations on December 24 that year, quickly followed by 97 Squadron at Woodhall Spa, but the first operational sorties carried out by Lancasters did not take place until the night of March 3-4, 1942.

By the time that 617 Squadron was formed, specifically for the Dams Raid, on March 21, 1943, the Lancaster had been operational for just over 12 months and there were 18 operational Lancaster

squadrons in Bomber Command with some 300 aircraft on their strength. At 1943 prices, each Lancaster cost approximately £50,000 (about £1.5 million in today's money). Many Lancasters had already been lost on bombing raids and some in accidents, and although new aircraft were rolling off the production lines almost daily they were a precious resource. Air Chief Marshal Sir Arthur 'Bomber' Harris, the Commander-in-Chief of RAF Bomber Command, could not get enough of them and fiercely resisted any attempts to divert his precious Lancasters from his 'main force' bombing campaign against Germany to any other tasks.

He was not enamoured with the proposal that some brand new Lancasters should be denied to him for normal bombing operations while they were modified for a special raid that he pronounced had: "…not the smallest chance of working". "At all costs," he said, "stop them putting aside Lancasters and reducing our bombing effort on this wild goose chase." Gradually though, Harris was won over, partly by the influence of his deputy, Air Vice Marshal 'Sandy' Saundby, and eventually he was overruled, when the Chief of Air

Above: Lancaster ED817, the third prototype Type 464, was used for Upkeep trials at Reculver. It did not take part in the Dams Raid, but joined 617 Sqn afterwards.
(Author's Collection)

Sir Arthur Harris could not get enough Lancasters and resisted attempts to divert them from his 'main force'

Staff, Air Chief Marshal Sir Charles Portal, ordered that the raid should go ahead and that 30 Lancasters should be specially modified for it. In the event, only 23 Lancasters were actually converted, under the supervision of Roy Chadwick, being designated 'Type 464 (Provisioning)' Lancasters, a deliberately nondescript codename. The work was carried out at the Avro plant at Woodford in Manchester, where Lancasters were chosen from the production line at random and converted into Upkeep carriers.

THE TYPE 464 (PROVISIONING) LANCASTER

The Type 464s were Lancaster B.IIIs with Packard Merlin 28 engines, which at 1300hp each were slightly more powerful than the original Rolls-Royce engines. The main structure of the aircraft remained unaltered, but there were some significant modifications from standard Lancasters. The most obvious difference was the removal of the bomb bay doors, in order to accommodate the Upkeep, and the removal of the mid-upper turret to save weight. Even so, when the modifications were complete the Type 464 Lancaster weighed 1190lb more than a standard B1, even without the Upkeep bomb. The all up weight of the Dams Raid aircraft on take-off was 63,000lb (over 31 US tons or more than 28 metric tonnes).

BOMB BAY AND BOMB GEAR

The removal of the bomb bay doors and the alterations to the bomb bay to carry the Upkeep gave the Type 464 an ungainly appearance. It looked as though a large chunk had been cut from its belly.

When the specially-modified aircraft were subsequently delivered to Scampton, the ground crew, with typical service humour, named them "abortions". The bomb doors were replaced by front and rear fairings, which were added to the bomb bay to minimise drag as much as possible. In the gap between these fairing were mounted two V-shaped, hinged calliper arms to hold the Upkeep. These were made from rectangular-section metal tubing and hung from brackets attached to the bomb bay. At the bottom of the 'V' of each arm was a free-rotating disc, which mated with the support ring on the end-plates of the Upkeep. The calliper arms were sprung and the action of pressing the bomb-release 'tit' (as the RAF nicknamed such buttons), allowed the arms to spring outwards a few inches to release the weapon.

The motor for spinning the Upkeep was mounted in the forward part of the bomb bay. It was a Vickers-Jassey Variable Speed Gear (VSG) device that was used in submarines, but operating in the opposite sense on the Type 464 Lancasters. In submarines, the VSG was mechanically driven to pump hydraulic fluid to operate the control surfaces; on the Type 464 Lancaster it was powered hydraulically from one of the connections made redundant by the removal of the bomb doors and the mid-upper turret, and drove a large pulley which protruded from the right (starboard) side of the forward bomb bay.

A rubber V-belt ran from this pulley around the starboard calliper arm support disc to spin the Upkeep backwards at the required 500rpm. The motor speed and therefore the rpm of the bomb were controlled by the wireless operator using a valve

Below: Still showing its SECRET classification, this ground photo of Gibson's ED932 AJ-G loaded with an Upkeep bomb clearly shows the modified bomb bay (Crown Copyright)

mounted on the navigator's table. A rev counter taken from a motorcycle, driven from an attachment on the output shaft of the motor, showed the revolutions that the bomb was spinning at. This could be adjusted by turning the valve to allow more or less hydraulic pressure through to the motor. This arrangement could now be viewed as ingenious or rather Heath Robinson, but it worked.

ARMAMENT

The removal of the mid-upper turret meant that the two gunners who were part of the standard Lancaster crew of seven men, would occupy the rear turret (standard Fraser Nash FN-20 turret with four .303 Browning machine guns) and the front turret (FN-5A with two .303 machine guns). For normal 'main force' night operations there was no dedicated front gunner in a Lancaster (normally the bomb aimer doubled up as the front gunner, but on the Dams Raid he would be busy on the bombing run and there was an expectation of the need to suppress enemy anti-aircraft fire). Among the modifications subsequently added at squadron level were stirrups for the front gunner's feet, so that they did not dangle in front of the bomb aimer.

The earliest of the Lancasters to be converted were selected from the end of a production run that included fittings for a single Vickers K machine gun in the ventral position, and at least four of the Type 464s included these fittings. These guns were not generally fitted and were not manned or used on the raid itself due to the low-level nature of the operation, although it is believed that one Lancaster flew on the Dams Raid with the gun fitted. The spare aircraft ED825 AJ-T which was used by Joe McCarthy and his crew to attack the Sorpe dam, after their own aircraft went unserviceable on start-up, was only delivered to Scampton from Boscombe Down on the afternoon of May 16 and it still had the ventral gun fitted. This aircraft was later lost while being flown on a Special Operations Executive

(SOE) supply dropping operation from Tempsford on December 10, 1943. When the crash site was recently excavated, the ventral gun fittings helped to positively identify the aircraft.

OTHER MODIFICATIONS

One late change to the Type 464 configuration was the addition of the two Aldis lamps to assist the crews in flying at the correct bomb release height of 60ft over the water. This clever idea was the brainchild of Ben Lockspeiser, who was the director of scientific research at the Ministry of Aircraft Production. One of the lamps was fitted in the aircraft's nose underneath the bomb aimer's compartment in the place normally used for the bomb aimer's camera. This is visible in images of the Type 464 as a stub tube protruding under the aircraft nose, behind the pitot head. The other lamp was fitted in the rear bomb bay fairing. The two lamps were set to converge just forward of the wing leading edge and slightly to the right of the aircraft, to produce a 'figure of eight' on the surface below the aircraft when it was at exactly 60ft. The convergence could be viewed by the navigator from the Perspex blister on the starboard side of the cockpit glazing and he could then verbally control the height by telling the pilot to go "up" or "down".

The Type 464 Lancasters were fitted with the deeper bomb aimer's blister in the nose, which was gradually becoming standard on Lancasters. Some bomb aimers did not like using the wooden 'Y'-shaped sight with an eye hole and pins on the arms of the 'Y', which lined up with the towers of the dam to give the correct bomb release range. Some did use them, but others found it difficult to hold steady with one hand while the other gripped the bomb release 'tit'. An alternative method of judging the release range was

Above: An air-to-air shot of Type 464 ED817, after it joined 617 Sqn.

Below: ED825 AJ-T was used for trials prior to the Dams Raid then flown by Joe McCarthy on the mission. (both Author's Collection)

A motorcycle rev counter showed revolutions. This could be viewed as Heath Robinson, but it worked.

INDIVIDUAL HISTORIES OF ALL THE 23 TYPE 464 LANCASTERS PRODUCED.

D765: First prototype. To Farnborough April 8, 1943. Used for trials. Did not take part in the Dams Raid. Later coded AJ-M, it was lost in a crash at Ashley Walk bombing range, Hampshire, on August 5, 1943.

ED817: Second prototype. To Manston April 10, 1943, for Upkeep dropping trials at Reculver. Did not take part in the Dams Raid. To 617 Squadron April 30, 1943. Coded AJ-C and used occasionally for operations, trials and training duties. Scrapped September 23, 1946.

ED825: Third prototype. Delivered to A&AEE Boscombe Down April 22, 1943; then to 617 Squadron May 16. Coded AJ-T. Spare aircraft used by McCarthy on Dams Raid, attacked the Sorpe, landed safely. Shot down on December 10, 1943, on an SOE supply drop.

ED864: To 617 Squadron April 22, 1943, coded AJ-B. Astell's aircraft on the Dams Raid. Crashed after hitting electricity cables near Marbeck, Germany.

ED865: To 617 Squadron April 22, 1943, coded AJ-S. Burpee's aircraft on the Dams Raid. Crashed on Gilze-Rijen airfield, en route to target.

ED886: To 617 Squadron April 23, 1943, coded AJ-O. Townsend's aircraft on the Dams Raid. Attacked the Ennepe or possibly the Bever. Retained by 617 Squadron and used occasionally for operations, trials and training duties. Lost on an SOE supply drop on Dec 9-10, 1943 – crashed near Amiens, France.

ED887: To 617 Squadron April 22, 1943, coded AJ-A. Young's aircraft on the Dams Raid. Attacked the Möhne. Shot down on the way home, coasting out from Holland, crashed near Castricum an Zee.

ED906: To 617 Squadron April 23, 1943, coded AJ-J. Maltby's aircraft on the Dams Raid. Last aircraft to attack the Möhne. Retained by 617 Squadron and used occasionally for operations, trials and training duties. Stored at No. 46 MU from April 15, 1944. Delivered to 61 Squadron for Operation Guzzle in August 1946, coded YF-A. Scrapped July 29, 1947.

ED909: To 617 Squadron April 23, 1943, coded AJ-P. Martin's aircraft on the Dams Raid. Attacked the Möhne and landed safely. Retained by 617 Squadron and used occasionally for operations, trials and training duties. Stored at No. 46 MU from April 15, 1944. Delivered to 61 Squadron for Operation Guzzle in August 1946, coded YF-B. Scrapped July 29, 1947.

ED910: To 617 Squadron April 28, 1943, coded AJ-C. Ottley's aircraft on the Dams Raid. Shot down near Hamm en route to target.

ED912: To 617 Squadron May 3, 1943, coded AJ-N. Knight's aircraft on the Dams Raid. Successfully attacked and breached the Eder; landed safely. Retained by 617 Squadron, later recoded AJ-S and used occasionally for operations, trials and training duties. Scrapped September 26, 1946.

ED915: To 617 Squadron May 3, 1943, coded AJ-Q. Unserviceable on start-up for the raid and did not take part. Retained by 617 Squadron and used occasionally for operations, trials and training duties. Stored at No. 46 MU from February 1945. Scrapped October 8, 1946.

D918: To 617 Squadron April 30, 1943, coded AJ-F. Brown's aircraft on the Dams Raid. Attacked the Sorpe and landed safely. Retained by 617 Squadron and used occasionally for operations, trials and training duties. Crashed near Snettisham, Norfolk, during a night training flight on January 20, 1944, with a crew of four on board; two killed and two injured.

ED921: To 617 Squadron April 23, 1943, coded AJ-W. Munro's aircraft on the Dams Raid. Hit by flak coasting in over Holland – mission aborted and returned with Upkeep on board. Retained by 617 Squadron and used occasionally for operations, trials and training duties. Scrapped September 26, 1946.

ED924: To 617 Squadron April 30, 1943, coded AJ-Y. Anderson's aircraft on the Dams Raid. Mission aborted, returned with the Upkeep on board. Retained by 617 Squadron and used occasionally for operations, trials and training duties. Scrapped September 23, 1946.

ED925: To 617 Squadron April 30, 1943, coded AJ-M. Hopgood's aircraft on the Dams Raid. Shot down at the Möhne.

ED927: To 617 Squadron May 3, 1943, coded AJ-E. Barlow's aircraft on the Dams Raid. Crashed en route to the target after hitting electricity cables near Haldern, Germany.

ED929: To 617 Squadron April 30, 1943, coded AJ-L. Shannon's aircraft on the Dams Raid. Attacked the Eder and landed safely. Retained by 617 Squadron and used occasionally for operations, trials and training duties. Scrapped October 7, 1946.

ED932: To 617 Squadron April 30, 1943, coded AJ-G. Gibson's aircraft on the Dams Raid. Attacked the Möhne and landed safely. Retained by 617 Squadron, later recoded AJ-V, and used occasionally for operations, trials and training duties. Stored at No. 46 MU from February 7, 1945. Delivered to 61 Squadron for Operation Guzzle in August 1946, coded YF-C. Aircraft sustained Category 'AC' damage on take-off on Nov 11, 1946. Scrapped July 29, 1947.

ED933: To 617 Squadron May 3, 1943, coded AJ-X. The aircraft was splash-damaged dropping an inert Upkeep at Reculver during training for the raid on May 12 or 13. It was not repaired in time to be used on the Dams Raid. Later re-coded AJ-N and used for various trials. Scrapped October 7, 1946.

ED934: To 617 Squadron May 3, 1943, coded AJ-K. Byers' aircraft on the Dams Raid. Shot down coasting in over Texel, Holland.

ED936: To 617 Squadron May 12, 1943, coded AJ-H. Rice's aircraft on the Dams Raid. Hit the water and lost the Upkeep, mission aborted, landed damaged and sent away for repair. Returned to 617 Squadron and used occasionally for operations, trials and training duties. Scrapped July 29, 1946.

ED937: To 617 Squadron May 14, 1943, coded AJ-Z. Maudslay's aircraft on the Dams Raid. Attacked the Eder. Shot down near Emmerich on the return flight.

devised with a piece of knotted string attached across the bomb aimer's blister from left to right fastened by two of the bolts and then pulled back into a triangle against the bomb aimer's eye. Marks made on the blister perspex would then match the dam towers at the correct range.

The final significant modification to the Type 464 Lancasters was the fitment of fighter aircraft style TR1143 VHF radios, to allow voice communication between the aircraft in the target area, particularly between the leader, Wing Commander Gibson, and the other pilots. This would allow the leader to have instant control over the operation.

THE TYPE 464 AIRCRAFT HISTORIES

The first prototype Type 464 Lancaster, ED765, arrived at Royal Aircraft Establishment Farnborough for initial trials on April 8, 1943. The second, ED817, was sent immediately to Manston 12 days later for Upkeep drop trials. The third, ED825, was delivered to the Armament and Experimental Establishment at Boscombe Down for trials. The first Type 464 arrived with 617 Squadron at Scampton on April 8 and when more of the modified aircraft had arrived, it allowed the squadron to release the 10 standard Lancasters which they had been using for their low flying training so far, back to Bomber Command for redistribution to other units.

Of the 23 Type 464 Lancasters converted, 19 flew on the Dams Raid and eight of those were lost. After the raid none of the Type 464s were returned fully to standard Lancaster configuration as it proved too difficult or costly to refit the bomb bay doors. Some were used by 617 Squadron or other units, without their bomb doors, on bombing operations or for SOE supply drops. Two were lost on operations after the Dams Raid and two were destroyed in crashes. The remaining 11 Type 464s saw out the war in one

capacity or another and were then scrapped postwar. What the world would give today if one of them had been saved for posterity.

Three of the Type 464 Lancasters were recalled to Upkeep carrying duties between August and September 1946 for Operation Guzzle, the purpose of which was to dispose of the remaining Upkeep bombs left over after the war. Lancasters ED906, ED909 and ED932 were attached to 61 Squadron at Waddington during these months. They were probably operated by No. 1 Group Major Servicing Unit, which was based at Scampton, with aircrew drawn from 1 Group to make up the crews. It appears that the aircraft borrowed Scampton's Station Flight unit code letters and wore the codes YF-A, YF-B and YF-C. They flew several trips to drop the remaining Upkeeps into the deep Atlantic from 10,000ft in a drop zone centred on 56N 12W.

LAST WORD ON THE LANCASTER

The last word on the Lancaster and its role in Operation Chastise should go to Barnes Wallis.

In a letter to the aircraft's designer, Roy Chadwick, written a week after the raid, he wrote: "No one believed that we should do it. You yourself said that it would be a miracle if we did and I think the whole thing is one of the most amazing examples of teamwork and co-operation in the whole history of the war. May I offer you my very deep thanks for the existence of your wonderful Lancaster, for it was the only aircraft in the world capable of doing the job, and I should like to pay my tribute of congratulation and admiration to you, the designer."

Above: Gibson's Lancaster ED932 AJ-G during trials at Reculver. (© IWM FLM 2354)

"It was the only aircraft in the world capable of doing the job."
Barnes Wallis

Opposite page: Type 464 ED906 was David Maltby's aircraft on the Dams Raid. It survived the war and was used in 1946 for Operation Guzzle to dispose of left-over Upkeeps. It is seen here at Waddington during that operation with postwar style serial letters under the wings and code letters YF-A. (Author's Collection)

The Leader

Wing Commander Guy Gibson VC DSO* DFC*
"A man born for war... but born to fall in war"

* with Bar

To the general public, the name of Guy Gibson is perhaps one of the best known of all RAF airmen, mainly because of his leadership of the legendary Dams Raid in 1943. Over the 70 years since that event, myriad books, films, TV programmes and feature articles have added to the public knowledge of Guy Gibson's part in the raid itself and why he was so deserving of the supreme British award for gallantry – the Victoria Cross (VC).

Relatively little, though, about the rest of his life and career and about his character and personality has been widely published or broadcast. Indeed, most people's ideas of what Gibson was like as a person are probably based on the portrayal of him by the extremely well cast Richard Todd, in the famous 1955 film The Dam Busters.

Guy Gibson really was a hero in the true sense of that word, which is much overused today, but which in the Oxford Dictionary is defined as: 'man of superhuman qualities... illustrious warrior'. His influence on the motivation of those around him, and especially on those who flew on Operation Chastise, was enormous. In actuality though, he was no angel and, although he was undoubtedly a role model to many, he had flaws in his character, as most human beings do. So what was he really like and what of those aspects of his character and personality which are less well known? To start to answer that question we need first to explore his background and earlier career.

Guy Penrose Gibson was born on August 12, 1918 at Simla in northern India, the son of Nora and Alexander J Gibson, who was a colonial officer in the Imperial Indian Forest Service and a specialist in the industrial extraction of turpentine and other chemicals from timber products.

The Gibsons were a dynasty of engineers and technocrats who had perpetuated a family tradition of training and marrying at home in England, migrating abroad to work in industry while raising their families, and then retiring to Britain in middle age.

Guy Gibson's grandfather had worked in Russia and Alexander Gibson, Guy's father, had been born in Moscow, he was educated in England and then studied forestry before joining the Indian Forest Service. He was 18 years older than his wife, Nora, who was just 19 when they married and 23 when Guy, her second son and the youngest of three children, was born. Alexander Gibson was aloof and remote, emotionally distant from his wife and his children, and Guy probably never really knew him. At six years old, like most colonial children of the time, Guy was sent to England so he could attend boarding school. Thereafter he had little more to do with his father.

Guy's mother accompanied him to England and remained, as her marriage was already failing. Having become used to the privileged life of a colonial wife in India, Nora Gibson became increasingly lonely, depressed and volatile; sadly, she became dependent on alcohol. She was unable to provide the stability that her three children needed, especially Guy as the youngest, and they were starved of parental support and affection. When Guy was 14, his mother was even jailed briefly for a series of drunken driving offences.

After that, Guy had little more to do with her and tragically Nora died in 1939, at Christmas time, as a result of horrific burns sustained when her nightdress caught in an electric fire. After attending prep school in Folkestone, Kent, Guy was sent to St Edward's School in Oxford, a lesser public school, where the muscular discipline would have been good preparation for life in the services. Although no more than average in academics, he was a good sportsman and displayed, it was reported, "a very determined attitude". Whatever else Guy Gibson gained from his schooling, it gave him unshakeable confidence and self-belief. During school holidays, with no real family of his own, Guy was passed from one relative to another, although he spent more time with his maternal grandparents in Cornwall. Here, at least, there was an element of emotional stability. Even so, with the childhood he experienced, Guy Gibson had inevitably become emotionally hardened even if he was not perhaps exactly emotionally scarred.

On leaving school Gibson decided that he wanted to fly and in 1935, displaying his self-belief in abundance, he applied to Vickers Aviation for a job as a test pilot. He was tactfully advised to join the RAF to gain some experience, not to mention some training, first. Gibson took the advice, but was initially rejected by the RAF due to his small stature. Undeterred, he reapplied and was accepted, commencing his flying training with the Yatesbury civil flying school on November 16, 1936. He was commissioned as an Acting Pilot Officer on January 31, 1937, and moved to No 6 Flying Training School in February for advanced instruction. When he graduated from flying training in September 1937, almost exactly two years before war was declared, he was posted to 83 Squadron at Scampton, to fly the unit's Hawker Hind biplane bombers.

Above: Guy Gibson with his wife Evelyn in 1944. They were a 'golden couple' for the wartime propaganda machine. (© PA Images)

Rare, early colour photo of a Handley Page Hampden of No 455 Sqn RAAF, the type flown by Gibson from 1938 to 1940. (Crown Copyright)

In September 1938 the unit began to receive some Bristol Blenheims to use in conversion training for its imminent re-equipment with the new Handley Page HP.52 Hampden twin-engine medium bomber, which was already being delivered to its sister squadron, No 49, at Scampton. The newest of three medium bombers for the RAF – the others being the Armstrong Whitworth Whitley and the Vickers Wellington – the Hampden had been conceived as a fast manoeuvrable 'fighting' bomber, but with a maximum speed of 265mph it was no match for the latest Luftwaffe fighters and was really unsuited to modern air warfare. The Hampden had a crew of four (pilot, navigator/bomb aimer, wireless operator and rear gunner) and its cramped crew conditions earned it the nickname 'flying suitcase'. By the end of 1938 both 49 and 83 Squadrons had re-equipped with the Hampden and Gibson was qualified on type.

When war was declared on September 3, 1939, Gibson had been an officer in the RAF for over two and a half years and he was a relatively experienced bomber pilot. During the prewar years the RAF was quite rigid with its discipline and there was a high degree of rank consciousness both upwards and downwards. It is probable that Gibson carried some of these peacetime RAF attitudes into the war, as did others with prewar experience of the service, even though many in the wartime air force became less formal in these respects.

83 Squadron went into action on the very first day of the war, conducting an unsuccessful sweep of the North Sea in search of the German fleet. There then followed a period of inactivity and Gibson's first effective operational sortie of the war was not flown until April 11, 1940, to 'sow' mines. From then until September 26, he flew a further 27 operational sorties over Germany, being awarded his first Distinguished Flying Cross (DFC) on July 8, 1940. The dangers of these early wartime bombing missions in aircraft unsuited to the task cannot be overstated. Almost half

(714) of the Hampdens built were lost on operations during the first two years of the war, taking with them 1077 crew killed and another 739 missing. Guy Gibson was fortunate to survive this early period on operations, but he seemed to have developed a taste for it and when he was sent on a rest tour as an instructor at the end of September 1940, he agitated for a return to operational flying.

On November 13, 1940, Gibson was posted to 29 Squadron, a night fighter unit, as a flight lieutenant, to command A Flight. The unit had just started to receive its first Bristol Beaufighters, although it was February 1941 before the squadron was fully equipped with the new night fighters. It was also in November 1940 that Guy Gibson married Evelyn (Eve) Moore, a beautiful chorus girl and dancer who, at 29, was eight years his senior; they had met at a party in Coventry during early December 1939 while Gibson was on leave and he had become infatuated with her. After they married Eve did not spend much time by her husband's side, usually living away from his bases, which were in rather remote parts of the country, while he lived in the Officers' Mess. Gibson's life as an operational pilot was too far removed from hers and he found himself unable to talk to his wife about his experiences. Eve was later to say that she never really knew her husband as he kept his innermost thoughts to himself. She said: "His first love was the Air Force and he was married to whatever aircraft he happened to be flying at the time. I only came second."

Flying from Wellingore, in Lincolnshire, 29 Squadron spent some months training and then conducting operational night patrols with their new

He missed the camaraderie of an operational squadron and was driven by an urge to prove himself.

Above and below: Maggie North, an RAF nurse who became Gibson's soul mate. (Pictures courtesy Yvonne Masters)

radar-equipped Beaufighters. Gibson's first night kill came on March 12, 1941, when, with Sergeant R H James as his observer, in Beaufighter R2246, he shot down a German Heinkel He 111 bomber near Skegness. Two nights later he claimed another Heinkel 111. On April 8, 1941, when returning to Wellingore after an uneventful night patrol, Gibson's Beaufighter was attacked by a German Junkers 88 night intruder, as he was landing. The Beaufighter crashed through a hedge and the aircraft was damaged beyond repair; Gibson escaped unscathed, although he must have been shaken, but his observer, Sergeant Bell, was injured. At the end of April 1941, the squadron moved to West Malling, Kent, and for the next eight months Gibson flew operational night patrols from there, being promoted to squadron leader in June. He claimed a Ju88 shot down in flames on May 3-4 and on July 6 he downed another He 111 near Sheerness. Gibson was awarded a Bar to his DFC on September 10, 1941 (his radar operator for all his kills, Sergeant RH James, was awarded a DFM). By December 1941, Gibson had flown 99 operational sorties in Beaufighters and his victory tally was three enemy aircraft destroyed, one probably destroyed and four damaged (all at night).

Gibson was then sent on a rest tour as the chief instructor at the Beaufighter Operational Training Unit at Cranfield, but again he hankered to get back on bomber ops. For him, being an instructor was a kind of purgatory. He missed the camaraderie of an operational squadron and he seemed to be driven by a compelling urge (quite unreasonably) to prove himself. Also it did not seem right to him that many of his friends were in harm's way and paying the price with their lives, while he was relatively safe as an instructor. His wish was granted after only four months of instructing, not least because Air Marshal Harris had just taken over as Commander-in-Chief at Bomber Command; he knew Gibson and believed that his cool imperturbability coupled with his 'press on' attitude was exactly what he wanted in his senior bomber pilots and commanders. Besides, when Harris had been Air Officer Commanding (AOC) 5 Group, he had promised Gibson that once he had done his time on night fighters he would get him the best job he could.

So, on April 13, 1942, still aged only 23, Gibson was promoted to wing commander and posted to command 106 Squadron at Coningsby (the unit moved to Syerston on October 1). The squadron was equipped with the troublesome Avro Manchester until June 1942, but began to receive the much more capable Lancaster in May of that year, not long after Gibson arrived. Gibson was now in command of 18 ever-changing crews and some 500 men. For the next 11 months the youthful Guy Gibson led the squadron with great energy and moulded it into one of the best units in Bomber Command. Leading from the front he participated in most of the major raids flown during that period, personally completing another 46 ops, when the normal operational tour was 30 ops – which few survived. This brought his total operational sorties to an amazing 173 by the end of his tour. Gibson was awarded the DSO on November 6, 1942, and a Bar to his DSO followed on March 30, 1943.

Those who worked under him on 106 Squadron revered his professionalism and his ability to inspire confidence and to motivate, but they also found him to be tough, brash and often aloof, a strong disciplinarian with a certain amount of arrogance, no doubt born of his confidence in his own ability as one of the most experienced operational bomber pilots in the RAF. His uncompromising attitude was shown with his own crew when after several sorties he decided that two of them were sub-standard and immediately had them replaced. Meanwhile when a visiting Air Ministry team suggested that his rear gunner (Pilot Officer John Wickens) was too tall at 5ft 11in, Gibson told them to forget it, his gunner was staying. Socially, Gibson was a gregarious 'party animal', at least in the Officers' Mess. He made a point of drinking with his officers and joining in with games and sports. On duty though, he imposed strict, almost obsessive discipline, believing this to be essential to a fighting unit. He stood up for his men against any outside criticism, backing them to the hilt, but would come down hard on anyone who deviated from his rules and ethos; he was, in fact, a decidedly autocratic leader, but very much the leader.

Although, outwardly, he appeared immune to it, the strain of being on operations and the loneliness of command did affect Gibson and there were few people he could confide in or seek advice from. One person who provided him with support and friendship was the 30-year-old station commander at Syerston, Group Captain Gus Walker DSO DFC. Gibson both greatly liked and respected his station commander, who eased his administrative burden enormously. He was also the

one person to whom Gibson was willing to defer; no one else was allowed to question his decisions regarding the running of his squadron.

On December 8, 1942, Gibson and Walker were watching aircraft taxiing out to take off on a raid, when the station commander noticed through his binoculars that a stationary Lancaster from 61 Squadron had its bomb bay doors open and that incendiaries were dropping out and some were igniting beneath it. Worried that this might set off the 4000lb 'cookie', which was probably hanging in the bomb bay, he dashed to his car and drove off to warn the crew. Gibson saw him get out of his car about 20 yards from the aircraft and wave his arms, then the 'cookie' exploded and the Lancaster just disappeared. The tremendous blast blew Gus Walker 200 feet backwards, he should have been killed, and as Gibson raced to the scene he feared the worst, but in fact Walker had survived, albeit with the loss of his right arm which was blown off by the force of the explosion. Walker was taken to the RAF hospital at Rauceby, near Cranwell in Lincolnshire, where he was tended by, among others, a young and attractive RAF nurse, Corporal Maggie North. When Gibson visited Walker in the hospital the next day he spent some time talking with Maggie and was obviously quite taken with her. After hearing from her about the many burns victims that were dealt with in the hospital and her part in their care, he asked Maggie out for a drink on an impulse. Although Gibson was already married to Eve, he recognised in Maggie someone who had come face to face with the daily violence, traumas and fears experienced by bomber crews, including himself,

someone who understood and with whom he could open up and be himself. Reluctant at first, because Gibson was already married and also because of his rank (he was a wing commander and she a mere corporal), Maggie North was flattered by his attention and drawn to this complicated man, whose moods swung between high spirits and wistful fragility.

A series of dates followed, as an intense relationship developed between Guy and Maggie, albeit one that was still entirely platonic. Gibson no longer had his friend Gus Walker to support him and in Maggie he had found someone else he could talk to, openly. He and Maggie spent the next few weeks dashing around the local countryside in his car, enjoying secretive trips to the movies and to local pubs. They had to conduct their meetings in secret for fear of causing a public scandal, as Gibson and his wife Eve were the subject of considerable media attention, a 'golden couple' for the wartime propaganda machine. For both Guy and Maggie this was a form of escapism from the very real stresses of their wartime working lives and their happiest moments were spent planning a fantasy future life together in an imaginary cottage they called 'Honeysuckle Cottage'. One day in January, four days after he had lost two of his best crews and several of his close friends over Essen, Gibson appeared at Rauceby hospital unannounced,

Above: Guy Gibson, as OC106 Sqn, celebrating with aircrew after the RAF's first 1000 bomber raid against Cologne in May 1942. Some of the unit's Avro Manchesters are in the background. (© IWM ZZZ6965C)

He stood up for his men against any criticism but would come down hard on anyone who deviated from his rules.

as he often did. The night before, he had been on a difficult trip to Berlin and he looked completely 'washed out'. A nursing sister, who had seen that look before, found Maggie North and told her that she had better go to him. She found him sitting in his car, staring through the windscreen into the distance, shaking uncontrollably. She held him in her arms until the shaking stopped; he did not discuss or explain this nervous breakdown any further and it did not happen again.

This event shows that Guy Gibson was obviously a very human individual who was vulnerable to the stresses and fears that he had to face on a daily basis and which many others would not be able to endure for even short periods. His brief breakdown, after which he never wavered in his desire to continue on operations whatever the risks, does not make him less of a man but even more of a hero for continuing. As time went on it became obvious to Maggie North that the relationship between her and Guy had no long-term future. She knew that he would never leave his wife Eve for her, even though their marriage was broken and he was lonely and unhappy. So, just three months after their first meeting, Maggie married another man (a marriage that was doomed to fail). Gibson visited her on a few occasions afterwards, but this was to be a sad, unrequited affair.

When Gibson's tour as OC 106 Squadron ended in mid-March 1943, he was tired, exhausted even, and probably suffering from what we today recognise as combat stress. His last operation with 106 Squadron had been a difficult and stressful one, longer than planned after the port outer engine failed over Germany on the way to the target – which was Stuttgart – and he had to fly lower and slower than the rest of the bomber stream after the crew decided to continue the mission on three engines. He was now due some well-deserved leave and a rest. However, much to his dismay, his leave was cancelled and Gibson was called to the group headquarters where he was asked by the AOC, Air Vice Marshal Cochrane, if he would do one more 'special' operation. The senior air-rank officers had no doubt Gibson was the man for the job and his sense of duty and patriotism meant he was never going to refuse.

The new squadron which was put together specially for the operation and which he was to lead – 617 Squadron – was officially formed on March 21, 1943. From then until the Dams Raid took place was a mere 56 days.

Above: Guy Gibson with his beer-drinking black labrador dog.
(Author's Collection)

Below: Guy Gibson from his 106 Sqn days, flanked by his flight commanders: Sqn Ldr J H Searby (left) and Sqn Ldr P Ward-Hunt. Gibson's Lancaster B1, ED593 is behind them.
(© IWM HU91942)

The responsibilities, the efforts and the strains that Gibson had to contend with to set up a brand new squadron and complete its training for a unique low level night operation, in that timescale, should not be underestimated. Although he had plenty of help from other members of the squadron, from others at Scampton and from those above when things needed to be given priority, it was still his responsibility. Gibson brought exactly the same style of leadership to the new unit that had employed on 106 Squadron. He ran roughshod over bureaucracy, he did not suffer fools gladly and he remained a tough, strict disciplinarian who demanded things be done right.

By this stage of the war, Gibson was running on a short fuse, which was hardly surprising, and he sometimes appeared arrogant, even aggressive and never showed much in the way of sentiment or sympathy towards anyone. For the officers with whom he socialised in the mess, where he could be the life and soul of the party, he was not only a respected leader but also someone they admired and even liked. His beer-drinking black Labrador dog was also part of his persona, adding an air of informality, and it quickly became an unofficial squadron mascot.

However, for the NCO aircrew, for whom Gibson was a more remote personality, only seen on duty, he was less easy to like. But they respected him for his record and they knew where they stood with him. He was very much the leader, charismatic, leading by example and carrying all along with him with unshakeable self-belief and confidence.

It is easy to forget that he was still only 24.

During the period of training leading up to the raid, Gibson was often called to meetings in Grantham at the group HQ or in London, or to observe trials of Upkeep so he had to leave much of the day-to-day

running of the squadron and its training programme in the hands of his flight commanders, Squadron Leaders Young and Maudslay. The draw on his time from these other commitments gave him a problem in completing his own training and that of his new crew to the required standard. This placed him in the position of having to work longer and harder than anyone else, adding to his fatigue. As the date for the raid drew closer, he alone, of the aircrew on the squadron, knew the targets and he was not able for security reasons to confide or discuss the details with any of them. He was also missing the company of Maggie North, not that he would have discussed classified information with her of course; his wife was far away and he must have felt the loneliness of command deeply. Privately, Gibson was struggling with the immense pressure, from the many often conflicting demands on his time, from the responsibility resting on his still very young shoulders and from the strain of having to appear always the bullish, determined, super-confident squadron commander. He was not getting enough sleep or rest and the strain was beginning to show; he was becoming increasingly irritable and bad-tempered, a boil had developed on his face and he had painful gout in his feet, afflictions brought on by stress and fatigue. The Scampton medical officer recommended that Gibson take two weeks off, which was out of the question; Gibson laughed in his face and carried on. He did manage to meet up with Maggie – now Mrs Maggie Figgins – early in May, at his instigation. They had not seen each other since before her wedding. They met in the pub they had used frequently and went on into Grantham to watch a film. Gibson obviously enjoyed this time with Maggie, it was a break from everything else and although he gave no

indication of what was on his mind or what was about to happen, it may have been a life-saver for him.

The evening before the raid, Gibson was in the station commander's house at Scampton with the Station Commander, Group Captain Whitworth, Barnes Wallis and the squadron's senior aircrew to discuss the details of the planning for the raid the next night. The meeting did not break up until midnight and as they were leaving to go to bed, Gibson was told that his dog had been killed, run over by a car outside the main gates of the camp. He put on a brave face and showed no emotion, but he must have been shaken by the loss of his loyal friend. He went back to his room alone and later admitted to feeling very depressed as he tried to get to sleep.

On the morning of the raid Gibson awoke at 5.30am having had no more than five hours' sleep and with the gout in his feet giving him considerable pain. Throughout the remainder of the day he had barely a moment's rest with all the preparations and activity for the raid that night. He presided over the briefings to the pilots and navigators at noon and to all the crews at 6pm when he spoke for the best part of an hour, standing the whole time, despite the pain in his feet from the gout. When Gibson boarded his aircraft AJ-G and was asked to pause for the now famous photograph of him and his crew, he had been awake and fully occupied for over 15 hours. In the photograph he is wearing his German life jacket over his shirt with sleeves buttoned down, his hair is

Above: Guy Gibson and his crew boarding their Lancaster for the Dams Raid – on the evening of May 16, 1943. From left: Flt Lt Richard Trevor-Roper, Sgt John Pulford, Plt Off George Deering, Plt Off Fred Spafford, Flt Lt Bob Hutchison, Guy Gibson and Plt Off 'Terry' Taerum. (© IWM CH18005)

"In another minute we will all be dead... this is terrible – this feeling of fear – if it is fear."
– Guy Gibson

neatly groomed and he appears calm and relaxed with a trace of a smile on his face. There is no clue as to what he may have been feeling or of the fatigue he must have been suffering.

Guy Gibson's action on the Dams Raid itself are well documented elsewhere, but it is worth highlighting that he was the first to cross into Germany at the extremely low level that the mission was flown at. He was also the first to attack the Möhne dam – captain of the first crew to drop an Upkeep bomb in anger – albeit without immediate effect. From then on, he exercised tight local control on the aircraft of the 'First Wave' in the role of what was subsequently to become known as Master Bomber. He experienced the ferocity of the flak on his own bombing run and it is clear from his own account in his book Enemy Coast Ahead (written in 1944 and first published in 1946) that he was not immune to fear. He wrote that he felt that it was a horrible moment on the attack run with the enemy tracer swirling towards him, "... we were being dragged along at four miles per minute, almost against our will". He admitted that at that moment he did not want to go on, believing that: "In another minute we will all be dead... this is terrible – this feeling of fear – if it is fear." His doubts as to whether he could possibly survive the moment were voiced in his words to his flight engineer, Sergeant Pulford: "Better leave the throttles open now and standby to pull me out of the seat if I get hit." It is even more amazing, therefore, that having experienced the fear of imminent death from the enemy flak and miraculously survived, and then having witnessed the next aircraft to attack – Hopgood's – get shot down, that he opted to fly in alongside the third, fourth and fifth attackers to draw the enemy fire. That decision took sheer courage and it undoubtedly contributed to the successful breaching of the Möhne dam. When Gibson eventually landed safely back at Scampton after the raid he had been awake for almost 23 hours and then he needed to debrief, celebrate with the surviving crews and complete some administrative tasks before he could sleep.

After the Dams Raid, Guy Gibson and the Dambusters were lauded and he became a wartime celebrity. The King and Queen visited the squadron at Scampton on May 27, and on June 22 there was a mass investiture at Buckingham Palace when Gibson

Above: The graves of Wg Cdr Guy Gibson and Sqn Ldr Jim Warwick at Steenbergen, Holland. (Author's Collection)

received his VC from the Queen (the King was away in North Africa). The squadron's day out in London turned into quite a party. The AOC 5 Group, Sir Ralph Cochrane, was true to his word when he had asked Gibson to do just one more sortie and Gibson was stood down from operations and sent to Canada and the US on August 3, as one of Winston Churchill's entourage on an official visit. (Meanwhile, on July 2, 617 Squadron was given a new commanding officer, Squadron Leader George Holden who was soon promoted to wing commander.)

Gibson finally returned to Britain in December 1943 looking thin, drawn and exhausted and he was posted to a desk job and then to staff college. He returned to a semi-operational post as a staff officer at HQ 55 Base, East Kirkby, Lincolnshire, on June 12, 1944, with responsibility for operational planning and liaison. A couple of weeks after he arrived he wrote to Maggie and arranged to meet her in Bognor Regis, where she was now based. He had not seen her in nearly a year but their feelings for each other were still very much alive. After returning to East Kirkby, he wrote Maggie a card: "The day was perfect. I love you now and forever." On July 19 Gibson scrounged another operational sortie, piloting a 630 Squadron Lancaster on a daylight raid against a V1 site at Thiverny. Clearly, his desire to fly on operations was still not sated, indeed, he found being on an operational base without going on ops a sort of mental torture.

On August 2, Gibson was moved to HQ 55 Base at Coningsby. Still officially non-operational and in a ground post, he managed to fly three more individual operational missions – two during August in a P-38 Lightning on loan to the base for trials and operations, and a sortie to Le Havre on September 10 in a DH Mosquito on loan from 627 Squadron at Woodhall Spa – but his persistent requests for a full return to ops were firmly refused by higher authority. Finally, on September 19, 1944, Gibson was granted permission to fly one final op when he appointed himself as the Master Bomber for a raid on Rheydt, which was considered a 'soft' target. The raid was to consist of 220 Lancasters and 20 Mosquitos to mark and then bomb railway and industrial targets. Gibson piloted Mosquito B.XX KB267, E-Easy of 627 Squadron on only his second sortie in a 'Mossie', with Squadron Leader Jim Warwick DFC as his navigator on his first sortie on type. Gibson did not need to be taking these risks; indeed it was entirely unnecessary. His decision, fuelled entirely by his thirst to fly operationally again, had a tragic outcome. Gibson's aircraft failed to return from the sortie and it later became apparent that both he and Warwick had been killed when their Mosquito crashed near Steenbergen in Holland. Gibson was only 26 when he died.

It may never be known what really happened to Gibson, Warwick and their Mosquito. For many years it was assumed that they were shot down by enemy fire. After the war, an eye witness who had been on the ground near to the crash site on September 19, 1944, reported seeing an aircraft curving over Steenbergen, its engines both spluttering to a stop, before it became an arc of flames curving to earth and exploding on impact. This led many to wonder whether the inexperienced Mosquito crew had made an error with fuel tank selections, causing the engines to be starved of fuel. This theory did not explain the eye witness description of the aircraft catching fire before hitting the ground nor why there appeared to be no attempt at a forced landing.

However, in 2011 a new cause was forwarded to explain Gibson's death.

Newly uncovered evidence indicated that Gibson's Mosquito may have been brought down by what is now termed 'friendly fire'. Sergeant Bernard McCormack, a rear gunner in a Lancaster bomber returning from a raid over Germany, may have mistaken Gibson's Mosquito for a Junkers 88; he fired 600 rounds at it and shot it down. Once McCormack became convinced that he had shot down and accidentally killed Guy Gibson, he kept the terrible secret to his death. McCormack died in 1992 but, racked with guilt, he had given his wife a taped confession before he died, which was passed to researcher James Cutler. Cutler had previously unearthed a report in the National Archives by the crew of McCormack's Lancaster describing the incident. Another Lancaster crew flying in the same area as McCormack's also noted in their sortie report that they saw an aircraft flying out of control before crashing and that red target indicator flares exploded when it impacted the ground. Gibson's Mosquito had been carrying red flares and Gibson had earlier radioed that he could not drop them because of an equipment malfunction, so the flares would still have been on board when his Mosquito crashed. Both Lancaster reports put them just three minutes flying time from Steenbergen at the time. It all seems to tie together and may perhaps explain a mystery which has persisted for decades. James Cutler, for his part, declared himself "100% satisfied" that Guy Gibson was killed by friendly fire and "99.9% sure that he was shot down by McCormack's Lancaster".

Whatever the cause, Gibson's death was a tragic waste, but he was in many ways a rather tragic, although undeniably heroic, figure who was perhaps always destined to die on operations. Like all the greatest heroes, he was flawed. He could be arrogant, was something of a martinet and could be horribly opinionated. Some who worked, fought and lived with him thought the world of him; others found him insufferable. What is clear is that during the work-up training for the Dams Raid and on the operation itself, Gibson's achievements were herculean. Despite extreme mental and physical exhaustion, despite the

immense responsibility on his young shoulders, and despite being sufficiently unwell to warrant being grounded, he led the squadron with exceptional skill and bravery. He was a fearful man, yet overcame his fears with sheer courage. His flaws only make his achievement even more remarkable. Air Chief Marshal Sir Arthur 'Bomber' Harris, the Commander-in-Chief of Bomber Command, paid tribute to Gibson, saying that he was "as great a warrior as this island ever bred". Barnes Wallis, the astute and gentle scientist whose invention sent Gibson on his greatest exploit and who was horrified at the losses the squadron suffered, said this of Guy Gibson: "For some men of great courage and adventure, inactivity was a slow death. Would a man like Gibson ever have adjusted back to peacetime life? One can imagine it would have been a somewhat empty existence after all he had been through. Facing death had become his drug. He had seen countless friends and comrades perish in the great crusade. Perhaps something in him even welcomed the inevitability he had always felt that before the war ended he would join them in their Bomber Command Valhalla. He had pushed his luck beyond all limits and he knew it. But that was the kind of man he was... a man of great courage, inspiration and leadership.

"A man born for war... but born to fall in war."

Above: Portrait of Wg Cdr Guy Gibson in late 1943. (© IWM CH13618)

He was in many ways a rather tragic, although undeniably heroic, figure who was perhaps always destined to die on ops.

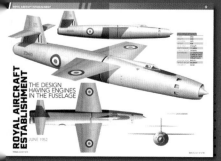

The Aircrew
SEVEN OF THE MANY

THE DAMBUSTER AIRCREW

One hundred and thirty-three brave men flew on Operation Chastise – the Dams Raid – on the night of May 16-17, 1943. They were a mixed group from a variety of backgrounds, cultures and countries, perhaps with little in common across the whole spectrum except for their boundless courage and a certainty that Nazism was evil and had to be defeated. 69% of the aircrew were from Great Britain, 21% were Canadian, and 10% were Australian or New Zealanders. There were 58 officers among the aircrew – all but three of the Lancaster captains were commissioned – but a greater number, the remaining 75, were NCOs. The youngest of the aircrew was only 18 years old and three, possibly four, were just 19. 65% of those who flew to the dams were between 20 and 25 years old, the most

common age being 21. The fact that few of them were over 25 is simply a reminder that in Bomber Command, the chances of survival beyond your mid-twenties were minimal. It is all the more remarkable, therefore, to find that 18 of the aircrew were aged in their thirties; the oldest being 35.

Eight of the 19 crews that set out on the raid did not return; 56 men were lost, 53 of them killed and three surviving to become prisoners of war. Of the 77 men who flew home from the raid, 32 of them were tragically to lose their lives later in the war and only 45 (34% of the original 133) survived to see the victory for which they fought.

Although the Dambusters were feted at the time and some were to become famous, the majority are not well known and, in many cases, did not receive any special recognition

or medals for their involvement in the raid. The crew of each Lancaster was seven men: pilot, flight engineer, navigator, wireless operator, bomb-aimer, front gunner (there was no mid-upper turret fitted to the special Type 464 Lancasters) and rear gunner.

The seven men whose stories follow, one from each aircrew specialisation, are among the less well known. They have been selected to provide a rough representative percentage of RAF, Royal Canadian Air Force (RCAF) and Royal Australian Air Force (RAAF) men, and a similarly representative cross section of the percentage killed on the raid, those killed later in the war and those who survived the war.

These are the stories of just a few of the real men who took part in one of the greatest feats of arms ever seen – Seven of the Many.

Dambuster aircrew survivors at a dinner hosted by A V Roe & Co Ltd at the Hungaria Restaurant on June 22, 1943.   (courtesy RAF Museum)

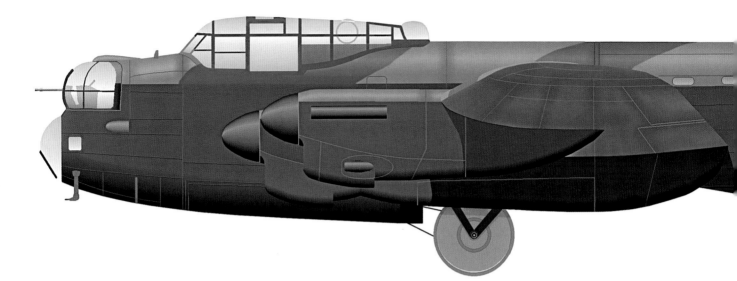

PILOT
Flight Lieutenant Harold 'Mick' Martin DFC (RAF)
(Lancaster ED909 AJ-P)

'Mick' Martin was one of the few Dambusters who survived not only the Dams Raid but also the entire war. Although his name is not as familiar to the public as those of Guy Gibson and Leonard Cheshire, he has been described by one eminent military historian as "one of the three great bomber pilots of the war".

Harold Brownlow Morgan Martin was born in 1918 in Sydney, Australia and had it not been for the war he would probably have followed his father into the medical profession. He left Australia in 1939, working his passage to England with the intention of studying medicine at Edinburgh University. In Australia he had been declared unfit to fly by the RAAF because of asthma, but when he got to England he applied to join the RAF, which accepted him in August 1940.

In the autumn of 1941 Martin joined 455 Squadron, flying Handley Page Hampden twin-engine medium bombers. This was the start of an apprenticeship that was to lead to him becoming one of the RAF's greatest wartime exponents of low level bombing. In these early days of Bomber Command's efforts to hit targets and avoid getting shot down, he quickly realised the effectiveness of low flying as a method of evading enemy fighters and flak, and he applied himself with relentless concentration to mastering the skills required. One night over Kassel he flew his Hampden so low that he hit a barrage balloon cable. Fortunately, the cable snapped and he flew away with it wrapped around one wing; he eventually got rid of it by diving to 50ft and getting it caught in a tree. In February 1942 he captained the first all-Australian crew to bomb Germany. One night his Hampden was hit by flak in several places and one engine was set on fire, but he managed to get back to base. After 13 operations, he and his crew moved to 50 Squadron, flying Hampdens, Avro Manchesters and then Lancasters on a further 25 ops. By the time that Mick Martin was rested from operations and sent to be an instructor at an Operational Training Unit in October 1942, he had built quite a reputation within Bomber Command for his low flying skills and expertise. He was awarded the Distinguished Flying Cross (DFC) the following month.

On March 31, 1943, Martin became the 20th pilot to join the newly formed 617 Squadron. As one of the most experienced 'on the deck' bomber pilots in the

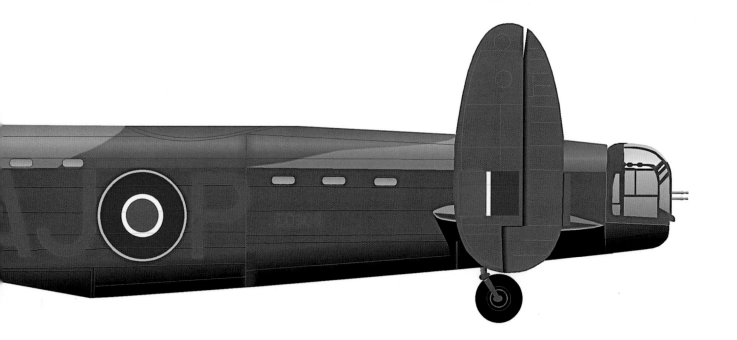

RAF he was a natural choice and Wing Commander Guy Gibson had personally asked him to join the new unit. The two had met during an investiture at Buckingham Palace when Gibson was there to receive a DSO and Martin his first DFC, and they had swapped notes on the merits of low flying. Martin was precisely the sort of experienced pilot that Gibson wanted for the forthcoming low level operation and to help train the other crews for the ultra-low-flying that was going to be required. Martin brought not only his low flying expertise to the squadron, but also his charismatic, extrovert and imperturbable personality. Although he tried to look older than he was by sporting a classic RAF airman's moustache, he was still only 23 when he joined 617 Squadron.

On the Dams Raid Martin flew as a wingman to Guy Gibson in the first three-aircraft formation of the 'First Wave', an indication of the CO's confidence in him. Martin's aircraft 'P-Popsie' was the third to attack the Möhne dam. On the attack run, as the Upkeep bomb was released, his aircraft was hit in the starboard wing by two anti-aircraft shells, one of which exploded in a fortunately empty fuel tank. Martin then flew in alongside the next two aircraft as they attacked the dam, to draw the enemy's fire and to provide suppression of the flak defences. He witnessed the amazing sight of the dam bursting after the last of these attacks, before being sent home by the leader, with his part in the night's actions complete. He landed safely back at Scampton at 3.19am after some 5 hours 40 minutes airborne.

After the raid Martin was awarded the Distinguished Service Order (DSO) for his actions. He was also ordered to report to the RAAF HQ in London to be interviewed by the Australian press, one of whom was an attractive, dark-haired Australian girl, called Wendy. He quickly lost interest in the required official 'line shoot' and asked his interviewer to lunch; she eventually became his wife when they married in October 1944. Martin remained with 617 Squadron, becoming a flight commander. When Gibson's successor as squadron commander, Wing Commander George Holden, was killed during the costly and abortive Dortmund Ems canal raid of September 16, 1943, Martin took over as leader and his was one of only three aircraft to return. He was awarded a Bar to his DFC and temporarily assumed command of the squadron until Wing Commander Leonard Cheshire arrived as CO in December 1943. Cheshire became one of the

squadron's most successful commanding officers with Martin as one of his stalwart flight commanders. Cheshire said of Mick Martin: "I learned everything I knew of the low flying game from Mick. He was the ideal wartime operational pilot. He had superb temperament, was quite fearless and innovative in his thinking. He was meticulous in his flying discipline and never did make a mistake."

Martin flew on most of the squadron's precision bombing raids until February 1944. On February 12, he was tasked with marking the target – the Antheor viaduct in the French Riviera – for the rest of the squadron to bomb. In typical style, he decided to run in at very low level, but encountered heavy flak and searchlights. One shell penetrated the nose of the Lancaster, hitting the bomb aimer, Bob Hay, in the head and killing him instantly; the flight engineer was also wounded in the legs. Martin landed his damaged aircraft in Sardinia. The crew had been together since the Dams Raid and Martin had promised them that they would all finish on ops together and so, with the sad death of their bomb aimer, this became his last, and 49th, heavy bomber sortie. He was rewarded with a Bar to his DSO.

Martin was rested from operations for a while, but he was impatient to get back, and got himself posted to fly DH Mosquitos with 515 Squadron on night intruder missions in support of Bomber Command's main force attacks. He flew another 34 operations with 515 Squadron, claiming two German night fighters shot down, three destroyed and one damaged on the ground during low-level attacks against German night fighter airfields. When he was finally removed from operations late in 1944, he had completed a total of 83 sorties over enemy territory. In November 1944 he was awarded another Bar to his DFC.

After the war, Martin remained in the RAF and had a long and immensely successful postwar career. On April 30, 1947, he set up a record for the flight from London to Cape Town in a Mosquito, covering the 6717 miles in 21 hours 31 minutes, at an average speed of 310mph. This feat gained him an Air Force Cross, and was not in fact surpassed until the jet age, when a Canberra bomber set a new mark. He rose up the ranks within the RAF, holding a number of staff appointments. He commanded 2nd Allied Tactical Air Force and RAF Germany from 1967 to 1970. He retired in 1974 as Air Marshal Sir Harold (Mick) Martin, KCB, DSO and Bar, DFC and two Bars, AFC. He died in 1988, aged 70.

Above: 'Mick' Martin as a Squadron Leader in 1943 wearing the ribbons of the DSO and DFC. He briefly commanded 617 Sqn at the end of 1943 after Wg Cdr Holden was killed in action. (Author's Collection)

Far left: Sqn Ldr 'Mick' Martin DSO and Bar, DFC and two Bars, with his DH Mosquito, prior to his record setting flight in April 1947. (© PA Images)

FLIGHT ENGINEER

Sergeant Robert 'Jock' Paterson (RAF) (Lancaster ED924 AJ-Y – Pilot Officer Anderson's Crew)

Not very much is known about Robert Paterson, but he is included here, with what detail is available, as the oldest man to take part in the Dams Raid and one of those survivors of the raid who was subsequently killed in action later in the war. Paterson was a Scotsman, born in Edinburgh, and a product of that most northern part of the United Kingdom that has produced so many of its finest warriors.

Like many other flight engineers, Jock Paterson started his RAF career as ground crew, joining up in 1938, before the war. His first posting after training was to 144 Squadron based at Hemswell, in Lincolnshire, where he worked on Handley Page Hampden bombers. A number of other ground crew postings followed, including some time spent working with Royal Navy aircraft at the Royal Naval Air Station at Lee-on-Solent and at Manston during 1942.

In late 1942, Paterson volunteered to become a flight engineer. Quite what made any man give up the relatively safe, if tough, environment experienced by RAF ground crew based in the UK, for the risks of flying on bomber operations over Germany, is hard to comprehend. Perhaps Paterson wanted to make a more significant contribution to the war effort, to make a difference, or perhaps it was simply for the excitement of flying. Whatever his reason, the die was cast and after training he found himself at the Heavy Conversion Unit at Swinderby, near Lincoln, to be integrated into a crew in his new specialisation of flight engineer. He and the rest of his all-NCO crew, captained by Flight Sergeant Cyril Anderson, then joined 49 Squadron at Fiskerton, Lincolnshire, in February 1943, to fly the Lancaster on operations.

Cyril Anderson was older than most bomber pilots at the time, aged 28 and married. Perhaps, with Paterson also being considerably older than most aircrew, at 35, and also married, the two had been drawn to each other in the crewing up process, where the RAF's procedure was to let everyone sort themselves into crews. By the third week of March, the crew had flown only five operational bombing sorties when they were posted to the newly formed 617 Squadron.

When Wing Commander Guy Gibson first started to form his new squadron, his criterion for crew selection was that they should have completed at least

one tour of 30 operations. However, it soon became apparent that this was not going to be possible to achieve across the board. Also it is not true that Gibson personally hand-picked all his crews for 617 Squadron. He chose some crews and individuals, but others either volunteered in response to a trawl sent out to squadrons or were sent to 617 Squadron by their station commanders. Anderson's crew, with Bob Paterson as their flight engineer, must have fallen into one of these two categories. They are certainly proof positive that not all the pilots and crews on the Dams Raid were experienced bomber 'aces'.

On Operation Chastise – the Dams Raid – the Anderson crew were part of the 'Third (Mobile Reserve) Wave' in Lancaster ED924 Y-York. As detailed elsewhere, they became hopelessly lost on the way to the target after veering well off track as a result of taking various evasive actions to avoid flak and searchlights. The GEE radio navigation signals were being jammed effectively by the Germans, mist was shrouding landmarks, the rear turret was playing up and dawn was beckoning. So at 10 minutes past three in the morning Cyril Anderson decided that

Right: Sgt Robert 'Jock' Paterson, Flight Engineer, and below: 'Jock's final resting place. (Author's Collection).

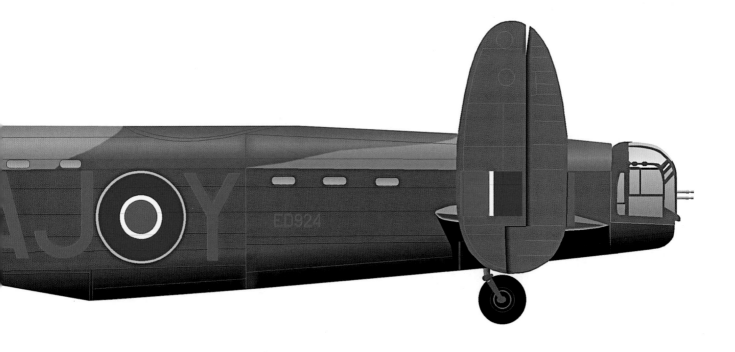

enough was enough, aborted the mission and turned for home. They landed back at Scampton at 5.30am unscathed, with the Upkeep bomb unused and perhaps a victim of their inexeperience for such a demanding low level mission. Gibson was not a man to sympathise with their predicament, however, and when he found out what had happened he was not best pleased. The Anderson crew was posted straight back to 49 Squadron.

Back with 49 Squadron at Fiskerton, the Anderson crew flew another 16 Main Force bomber operations, bringing their total to 22; just another eight to go to tour completion and a rest from ops. On September 23, 1943, they were sent on a night raid against Mannheim in Lancaster ED702. They bombed the target and were heading back towards home, somewhere near Offenbach, when they were attacked by a ME Bf110 night fighter flown by Lt Heinz Grimm. They probably never knew what hit them as they were attacked from below with the 110's Schräge Musik (steeply angled-up cannons mounted in the rear fuselage of some German night fighters). The Lancaster was hit in the petrol tanks; it was set on fire and exploded over Insheim.

All of the crew, including Bob Paterson, were killed. The bodies of five of the crew were recovered from the wreckage and buried in a local church yard at Offenbach. The other two members of the crew, who were probably blown out of the aircraft by the explosion, were found later and also buried with the others. They were subsequently reinterred at the Rheinberg British War Cemetery where they rest today. Their part in the raid may not have been glorious, but their courage cannot be questioned.

Above: Cyril Anderson's crew on 49 Squadron. From left: Robert 'Jock' Paterson, Jimmy Green, Doug Bickle, Arthur Buck, Anderson and John Nugent. (Author's Collection)

NAVIGATOR
Pilot Officer Torger Harlo 'Terry' Taerum (RCAF)
(Lancaster ED932 AJ-G – Wing Commander Gibson's Crew)

Torger Harlo 'Terry' Taerum was a farm boy from southern Alberta who had a vital role in the Dams Raid as the navigator in Guy Gibson's crew which led the operation. Gibson described him as his "great pal", with "a soft Canadian accent" and said that he was "probably the most efficient navigator on the squadron".

Taerum was born in Canada in 1920, the son of a Norwegian immigrant who established a farm near Milo, some 55 miles south of Calgary. Harlo Taerum was only 10 years old when his father was tragically drowned in Lake McGregor while attempting to save the lives of two boys who had fallen from their raft. After that, Taerum had a major role to play on the farm and in the upbringing of his two younger brothers and sister. Despite those pressures he excelled at school both academically and in sport as a track, baseball and rugby football star. Harlo had never visited Norway, but his father had often spoken to him about his beautiful homeland and when the Germans invaded and reports filtered back about their treatment of the Norwegian people, Taerum felt compelled to enlist in the RCAF, joining up in January 1941.

Below: 'Terry' Taerum (in the peaked cap) debriefing after Operation Chastise with Air Chief Marshal Harris (C-in-C Bomber Command) and AVM Sir Ralph Cochrane (AOC 5 Gp) standing behind. (© IWM CH9683)

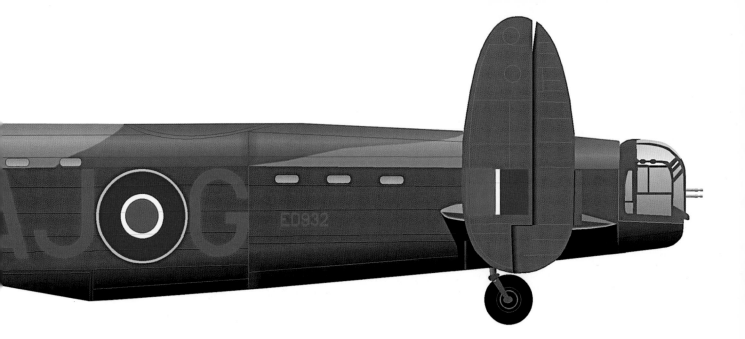

After completing navigator training in Canada, Taerum flew across the Atlantic as the navigator in a Lockheed Hudson, arriving in the UK to complete his training at Upper Heyford on Avro Ansons and Handley Page Hampdens. He then joined No 50 Squadron, flying his first operational sortie in a Hampden on January 2, 1942. It sounds as though it was a baptism of fire as he recorded in his log book against the sortie: "Caught in searchlights. Severely hit by flak." In March 1942 the squadron began to re-equip with Avro Manchesters and then with Lancasters. Taerum's first flight in a Lancaster was on May 14, 1942, but the squadron continued to operate the Manchesters alongside their newer, more capable Lancasters and Taerum's last operational sortie in a Manchester was flown on June 25. Assigned to the squadron's Lancaster conversion team as a navigation instructor, Taerum also continued to fly on ops. His last two operational sorties with 50 Squadron, both to Berlin, were flown with Flight Lieutenant 'Mick' Martin as his pilot.

It may well have been on Martin's recommendation that Taerum was posted to 617 Squadron and was selected to become part of Wing Commander Guy Gibson's new crew. (Gibson brought only one member of his crew with him from 106 Squadron – his wireless operator Flight Lieutenant Bob 'Hutch' Hutchison.) To have been hand-picked to be Gibson's navigator on 617 Squadron is probably the greatest compliment that could have been paid to a Bomber Command navigator at that point in the war.

When the Dams Raid happened on May 16-17, 1943, Terry Taerum was just a few days short of his 23rd birthday. His accurate navigation in the lead aircraft ensured that his aircraft stayed on track, avoiding flak hot spots, all the way to the Möhne dam. Subsequently his was the first aircraft to locate the Eder dam among the hills, in difficult, misty conditions. In all of this he was assisted by the bomb aimer, Pilot Officer 'Spam' Spafford, who used his roller map and checked for visual features through the Perspex blister in the aircraft nose. In a letter written to his mother in Canada after the raid, Taerum wrote: "It was by far the most thrilling trip I have ever been on and I wouldn't have missed it for anything."

After the raid Taerum was awarded the DFC and joined in the various celebrations that ensued. In another letter home he gives an insight into what that period was like for the survivors of the raid: "A couple of days later, five of us went to the factory where they

made Lancasters and gave the workers a pep-talk. Can you imagine me giving a speech? We were just about mobbed for autographs afterward. The next thing was five days of leave in London, and all the boys were down there, so we really had a time. At the end of five days, we were ordered back to our station to meet the King and Queen. They had lunch with us in the Officers' Mess and afterwards came out and inspected us. I was very lucky because I was introduced to both of them. The Queen is most charming and gracious. It really was quite a day."

Taerum remained on 617 Squadron after the Dams Raid and when Gibson left to go on his tour of Canada and the US, Taerum and three other members of Gibson's crew were taken on by the new commanding officer, Wing Commander George Holden. During his tour of Canada, Guy Gibson visited Calgary on September 11, 1943, and he was introduced to Terry Taerum's mother, Hilda Taerum. He told her that Terry was the living image of her and also said: "Terry is a great boy and a great navigator. He got the whole squadron to the dam." Tragically, four days after this happy and memorable event, Mrs Taerum received a telegram from the RCAF Casualties Officer: "regret to advise that your son flying officer Torger Harlo Taerum DFC J one six six eight eight is reported missing after air operations overseas september 15 stop letter follows".

On September 15, 1943, eight Lancasters of 617 Squadron, led by Wing Commander Holden with Terry Taerum as his navigator, had taken off from Coningsby for a special night low-level raid against the Dortmund-Ems canal. It was a very costly operation that achieved no success and only three of the eight aircraft returned to Coningsby. Holden's aircraft, with Taerum on board, was the first to be lost that night, shot down by light flak en route to the target at very low level. Others in the formation saw Holden's aircraft pull up to avoid a church steeple. As it did so, a burst of flak hit the Lancaster, setting one wing on fire, the fuel tanks exploded and the aircraft smashed into the ground near Nordhorn in a ball of flames. All of the crew, including the four Dams Raid survivors, were killed instantly. They are buried in the Reichswald Forest War Cemetery, Germany.

On February 3, 1945, Terry Taerum's younger brother Lorne Clifford was killed, when the 550 Squadron Lancaster in which he was a gunner, was shot down by a night fighter over Holland. He was 18 years old.

Above: 'Terry' Taerum – the 'great' Canadian navigator in Guy Gibson's crew. (Author's Collection)

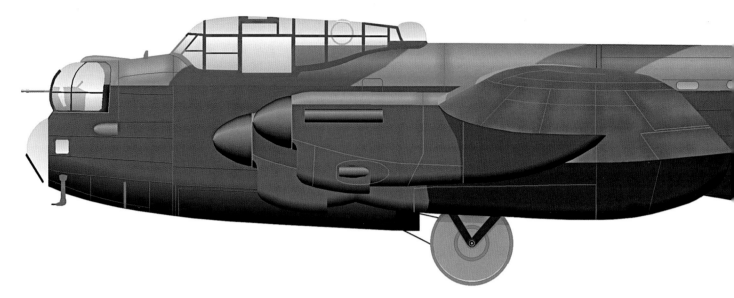

Below: Lancaster Type 464 – George Chalmers flew ops in all three types of the RAF's heavy four-engined bombers. (Author's Collection)

WIRELESS OPERATOR

Flight Sergeant George Chalmers (RAF)
(Lancaster ED886 AJ-O – Flight Sergeant
Townsend's Crew)

George Alexander Chalmers was born in 1921, at Peterhead in Scotland. He was educated at Aberdeen Academy and then worked briefly at a local Crosse & Blackwell factory before joining the RAF as a boy entrant in January 1938. On completion of his boy service and training as a wireless operator and air gunner, he was posted to 10 Squadron at Dishforth in Yorkshire in May 1939. After the outbreak of war he took part in leaflet-dropping operations over Germany in the squadron's twin-engine Armstrong Whitworth Whitley bombers.

In August 1940, Chalmers transferred to 7 Squadron, the RAF's first four-engine Stirling bomber squadron which was operating from Leeming. Three months later he was moved to 35 Squadron to fly operations in the four-engine Handley Page Halifax. During his service with 35 Squadron Chalmers was fortunate to survive an attack on the battle cruiser Scharnhorst at La Rochelle. His captain managed to bring the badly damaged aircraft back to base despite being severely wounded. In February 1942, after two and a half years on operations and having been 'mentioned in dispatches', Flight Sergeant Chalmers was 'rested' on instructional duties. In April 1943 he volunteered to join 617 Squadron for a special operation, becoming the wireless operator on Flight Sergeant Bill Townsend's crew. Flying in the Avro Lancaster with 617 Squadron meant that Chalmers achieved the rare feat of flying on operations in all three types of the RAF's heavy four-engine bombers.

On the night of the Dams Raid Townsend's O-Orange, with Chalmers aboard as wireless operator, was the penultimate Lancaster to take off from Scampton at 14 minutes past midnight. As the heavily laden aircraft climbed away from the short runway, Chalmers reckoned it brushed through the boundary hedge like a steeplechaser. As the aircraft headed across Holland and Germany at a mere 100 feet, Chalmers observed the Lancaster's progress from the astrodome on top of the fuselage next to his wireless operator's station. At one stage he was astonished when Townsend flew below tree level and along a fire break in a forest to escape enemy flak. En route to the dams, Chalmers received a radio message diverting O-Orange to the Ennepe dam. The crew had great difficulty finding the reservoir among the hills as the valleys were covered in mist, but they eventually released their Upkeep against what they believed was the Ennepe, unfortunately without success as it detonated short of the dam. Their return flight was an epic piece of low flying by pilot Bill Townsend, as dawn broke behind them, making them an all-too-visible target for the German flak gunners. As the aircraft coasted out at the Frisian Islands and the German anti-aircraft gunners depressed their guns to aim at the low flying Lancaster, Chalmers was amazed to see shells skipping off the surface of the sea and bouncing over the top of their aircraft. The aircraft was hit, but not fatally, although as they escaped out

> *The crew had great difficulty finding the reservoir among the hills as the valleys were covered in mist.*

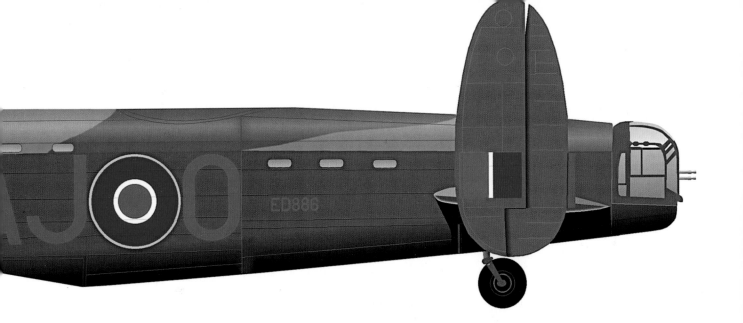

Chalmers was amazed to see shells skipping off the surface of the sea and bouncing over the top of their aircraft.

over the North Sea one of the engines developed an oil pressure problem and had to be shut down. They landed back at Scampton on three engines at 6.15am, the last of the 11 Lancasters that returned from the raid. Townsend was by now completely exhausted and, as he climbed down the ladder at the rear of the aircraft, he was asked by someone how it had gone. "Wait until debriefing," Townsend replied brusquely, completely failing to notice that his inquisitor was Air Chief Marshal Sir Arthur Harris, the Commander-in-Chief of Bomber Command.

Chalmers was awarded the Distinguished Flying Medal (DFM) for his part in the Dams Raid and for having flown 44 operational sorties. He was commissioned as a pilot officer in June that year and stayed on with 617 Squadron flying operationally with the unit until July 1944, by which time he was a Flight Lieutenant and had flown a total of 66 ops. For this feat he was awarded the DFC, the citation for which concluded: "Throughout his long and arduous operational career, this officer has displayed outstanding courage and devotion to duty."

In 1946 Chalmers was granted an extended service commission, and served postwar with 617 and 12 Squadrons until 1950, when he was posted to 38 Squadron, a Lancaster unit based in the Middle East.

He was released from the RAF as a flight lieutenant in 1954, and served in the Reserve until 1961. Meanwhile, he had joined the civil service at Harrogate, where he worked for the Ministry of Defence dealing with the RAF's technical requirements. In this period his advice was much valued in the sphere of flight refuelling, especially in relation to 'a refuelling system of outstanding value used by the RAF in the Falklands conflict'. George Chalmers passed away in August 2002 aged 81.

Above: George Chalmers, wireless operator, after he was commissioned and wearing his DFM ribbon. (Author's Collection)

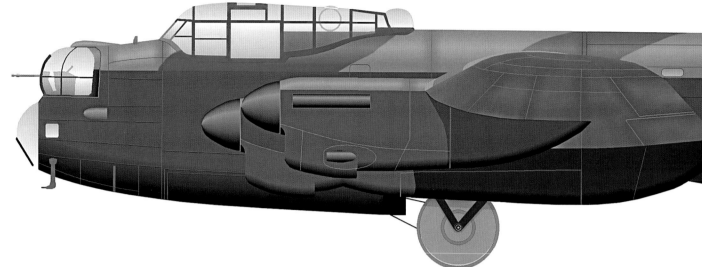

BOMB AIMER

Flying Officer Vincent MacCausland (RCAF)
(Lancaster ED887 AJ-A – Squadron Leader
Young's Crew)

Vincent Sanford MacCausland was born in February 1913 on Prince Edward Island, a small maritime province of Canada, situated in the Gulf of St Lawrence. As boy he was small for his age and tended to get bullied. After schooling he attended the University of Victoria in British Columbia and then became a teacher until he decided to join the RCAF in May 1940. He trained as an observer and subsequently as a bomb aimer in Canada and then in the UK. On completion of his training he was posted to 57 Squadron, based at Feltwell in Norfolk, flying Vickers Wellingtons. In September 1942 the squadron moved to Scampton and converted to Lancasters.

MacCausland completed a full tour of ops on 57 Squadron at a time when few survived that long. He was then sent to be an instructor at 16 Operational Training Unit where he flew in Wellingtons, training crews for night bomber operations.

In March 1943, now commissioned as a pilot officer, he returned to 57 Squadron at Scampton to fly in Lancasters for a second tour of operations. He became part of the crew of Squadron Leader Melvin 'Dinghy' Young DFC and Bar, a flight commander on 57 Squadron and a very experienced bomber pilot. When Young was recruited personally by Gibson to join the new 617 Squadron, as one of his flight commanders, he took his crew, including MacCausland with him.

In a letter home, written on April 17, 1943, MacCausland wrote: "You are perhaps wondering what I am doing here. There is really no need to feel over anxious to know that I am back again for my second tour. I really was due back six months after Sept of '41 but had the privilege of joining a well experienced crew and on aircraft that one dreams about. To tell you the honest truth I would not have taken this on had I believed it was a doubtful move. I came up here a couple of days ago (Apr 14) and we are on revision and conversion for the next month before going over with a few bundles for the 'squareheads'. I know that you will be feeling most

"I had the privilege of joining an experienced crew and on aircraft that one dreams about."
Vincent MacCausland

anxious during those few months ahead, but the time will soon pass and I know that God will be especially with us as were blessed in that first tour. I hope that we shall be writing at least two to three times per week and if you do the same, it will be much happier for us all."

On the Dams Raid MacCausland's Lancaster, A-Apple, with 'Dinghy' Young at the controls, led the second formation of the 'First Wave' to the Möhne. It was the fourth aircraft to attack the dam with MacCausland pressing the 'tit' to drop the Upkeep with extreme accuracy. The bomb caused a small breach and seriously weakened the dam so that the next aircraft to attack broke it. Young then took his crew on to the Eder as deputy leader.

On their way home though, the crew's luck ran out. As they coasted out across the sandy beaches at Castricum aan Zee on the Dutch coast, at extremely low level, within spitting distance of the open sea and relative safety, A-Apple was hit by flak. It plunged into the sea and on to a sand bar just off the coast with the loss of all seven crew members aboard. The bodies of Vincent MacCausland and the rest of the crew were washed ashore in late May 1943; they lie in Bergen General Cemetery in the Netherlands.

Buried far from home, his headstone reads: In loving memory. Faithful in Duty. Courageous in Battle. Brave in Death. At Rest.

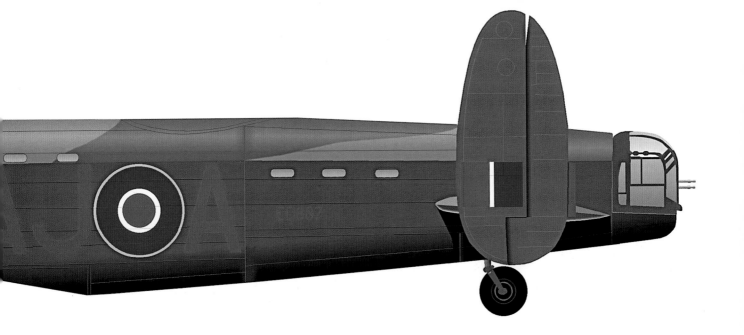

Above: On duty – Vincent MacCausland.

Above: MacCausland as a Sergeant in 1942. (both Author's Collection)

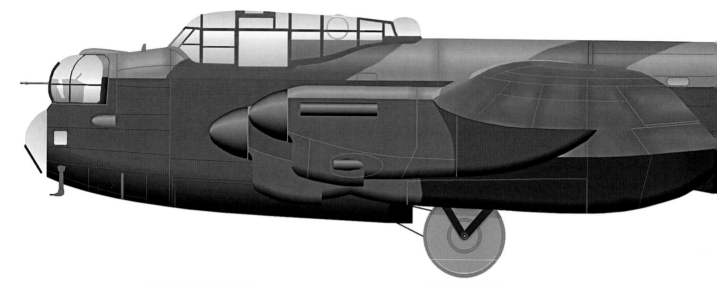

FRONT GUNNER
Flying Officer William John Tytherleigh DFC (RAF)
(Lancaster ED937 AJ-Z – Squadron Leader Maudslay's Crew)

Little is known of the lives of most of the gunners on the Dams Raid; it seems that in many cases they are almost forgotten members of the crews. 'Johnnie' Tytherleigh (sometimes known as Bill) was born in Hove, Sussex, in 1922. He joined the RAF as ground crew in April 1940, aged 18, and after training served briefly with 58 OTU, a Spitfire Operational Training Unit based at Grangemouth, near Falkirk in Scotland.

He then volunteered and was accepted for training as an air gunner, which he completed on Armstrong Whitworth Whitley bombers at 4 Bombing and Gunnery School at RAF Stormy Down, near Bridgend, South Wales. Now promoted to Sergeant, he was sent to 16 OTU at Upper Heyford to crew-up and to convert to Handley Page Hampdens, before joining 50 Squadron at RAF Swinderby in Lincolnshire. The Squadron moved to RAF Skellingthorpe in November 1941 and briefly operated the ill-fated Avro Manchester in April 1942, before it started to re-equip with Lancasters a month later. Tytherleigh, now an experienced air gunner, was commissioned as a pilot officer in May 1942 and in June the squadron moved back to Swinderby.

By the time that the trawl went out for crews to join 617 Squadron, Tytherleigh had completed a remarkable 41 operations and had been promoted to flying officer. He volunteered and was posted to the newly formed squadron on March 25, 1943, joining the crew of Squadron Leader Henry Maudslay DFC, as the front gunner. Maudslay was an old Etonian, still only 21 years old, but an experienced bomber captain with 40 ops to his name. He arrived on 617 Squadron on the same day as Tytherleigh and was appointed as one of the flight commanders.

Maudslay and his crew flew on the Dams Raid of May 16-17, 1943, in Lancaster ED937 AJ-Z, as part of the 'First Wave'; leading the last three aircraft of the wave. After the Möhne was breached, Z-Zebra went with the others to the Eder and they were the second

Right: 'Johnnie' Tytherleigh with his trademark pipe.

Far right: This picture of a group of 50 Squadron airmen was taken at The Parklands pub, Lincoln in June 1941. Tytherleigh is third from left.
(both Author's Collection)

> *'Johnnie' Tytherleigh was 21 when he died, the same age as his pilot. He is buried with his crew in a collective grave.*

to attack it. On their third attempt to get the almost impossible attack run right, the Upkeep bomb was released late; it hit the parapet of the dam wall without touching the water first and exploded on impact almost underneath their aircraft, which was most probably damaged as a result. The aircraft limped away, only faint and brief communication was heard from it, but it flew on at low level heading for home.

About 50 minutes after the crew of AJ-Z had dropped its bomb at the Eder they were 100 miles closer to home. Perhaps the aircraft was damaged or some of the crew were wounded, because the aircraft had strayed south of the planned return route and it flew directly over the heavily defended oil storage facilities at Emmerich am Rhein. At 2.36am Z-Zebra was engaged by the flak guns defending Emmerich and shot down in flames, crashing in a field to the north of the town near Klein Netterden. All seven men on board were killed instantly.

Johnnie Tytherleigh was 21 years old when he died, the same age as his pilot. He is buried along with the rest of his crew in a collective grave at Reichswald Forest Cemetery, Germany. Tytherleigh was awarded the DFC posthumously.

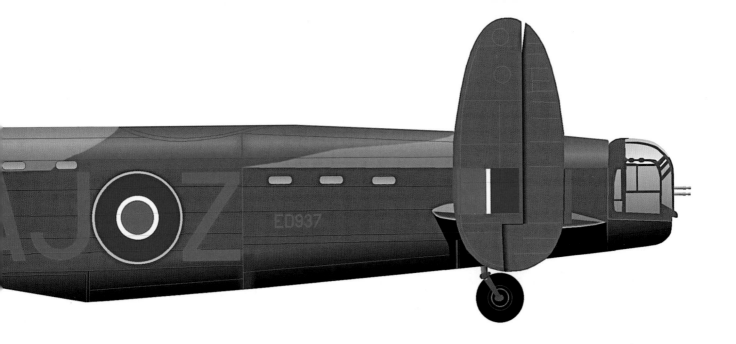

REAR GUNNER

Pilot Officer Anthony Burcher DFM (RAAF)
(Lancaster ED925 AJ-M – Flight Lieutenant
Hopgood's Crew)

Anthony 'Tony' Fisher Burcher was born in Sydney in 1922 and joined the Royal Australian Air Force in 1940. After training in Canada, where he qualified as an air gunner, he was promoted to sergeant in September 1941 and was posted to the UK.

In May 1942 he joined 106 Squadron at Coningsby, an Avro Manchester unit in the process of converting to Lancasters and recently placed under the command of Wing Commander Guy Gibson. Burcher went on to complete an eventful tour of operations, including a kill against a German night fighter, and he was awarded the DFM (gazetted April 20, 1943). Guy Gibson's original recommendation for the DFM stated: "Sergeant Burcher has completed a tour with 27 operational sorties, during which he has displayed the greatest enthusiasm and keenness. He has taken part in raids on German and Italian targets and mining sorties off France and in the Baltic, and flew as rear-gunner on the daylight raids on Danzig and Le Creusot. On July 29, 1942, his aircraft, returning from Saarbrucken, was attacked by five separate enemy fighters. Sound commentaries assisted his pilot to evade two of them, and his well-directed fire drove off another two and assisted in the certain destruction of the fifth. Sergeant Burcher, an Australian, has carried out his work with that cool courage and cheerfulness which well merits recognition." Burcher was commissioned as a pilot officer in November 1942 and in March 1943 he volunteered to join 617 Squadron.

"John Hopgood and Charlie Brennan stayed to the end... and I am alive because of it."
Anthony Burcher

At Scampton he was appointed as rear gunner in the crew of Flight Lieutenant John 'Hoppy' Hopgood DFC and Bar, another ex-106 Squadron man and a close friend of Guy Gibson. On the Dams Raid of May 16-17, 1943, the Hopgood crew flew Lancaster ED925 AJ-M as part of the first three-aircraft formation of the 'First Wave'. In an interview given some years after the war, Tony Burcher talked of his emotions before the raid. He said that he did not think he felt more worried than on any previous raid, but went on to say: "My mum used to send me malted milk tablets over to wherever I was posted. Like a lot of people in Australia, she had heard tales about us all starving in England. Poor old mum used to send Comforts Funds Parcels over to us and always enclosed a jar of malted milk tablets. I'd built up a store in my drawer in my quarters. I never took them with me on any trip before. In fact I had never eaten any of them before. But on the night of the raid I was walking down to the flight line with Brian Goodale, who was Dave Shannon's wireless operator and something prompted me to go back and pick up one of the jars of these tablets I had out of the drawer and put them on the inside pocket of my battledress. I don't know why. It was a feeling I had – a premonition I would need them. Later on, of course, when I was captured and hungry they came in very handy."

On the way to the target, with about 20 minutes to go, all three of the first 'vic' of Lancasters were caught by searchlights as they headed over Germany at very low level to the north of the Ruhr area. Hopgood evaded so violently that he flew underneath some high tension cables. Having apologised for this unscheduled manoeuvre, he climbed slightly and ordered Burcher to keep his eyes peeled. Moments later there were more searchlights and Burcher opened fire against them from his tail turret. His gunfire extinguished at least one of the searchlights, but the aircraft was raked by ground fire from nose to tail. A shell burst alongside the rear turret and Burcher was hit in the stomach and lower leg by shell splinters, injuries he later described as, "only scratches really". Things sounded worse at the front of the aircraft, though, where a shell had burst in the cockpit area. It became apparent that the front gunner Pilot Officer George Gregory had either been killed or mortally wounded, as nothing more was heard of him on the intercom when Hopgood called for the crew to check in. In addition, Burcher realised that the pilot, 'Hoppy' Hopgood, had been wounded in the head when the flight engineer, Sergeant Charlie Brennan, said: "What about your face? – it's bleeding like f***" and Hopgood replied: "Just hold a handkerchief over it." The Lancaster was also hit in the left wing, although not too seriously, and despite the damage and the injuries Hopgood decided that they should press on to the target, telling the crew: "I intend to go on because we've only got a few minutes to go.

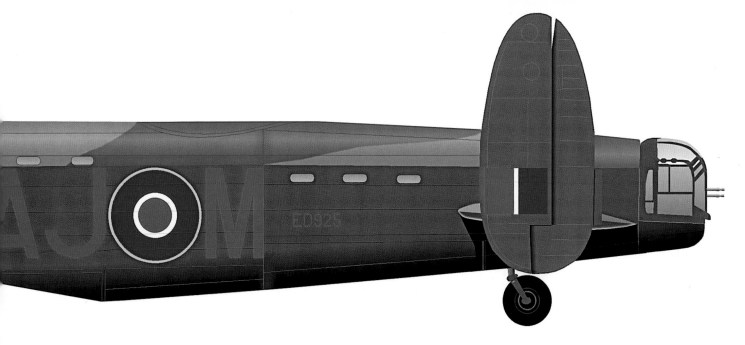

We've come this far. There's no good taking this thing back with us. I can handle the aircraft okay. So any objections?"

At the Möhne, after Gibson had dropped his Upkeep against the dam, apparently without effect, and the water had subsided from the explosion, he ordered Hopgood to be the second to attack. As they ran in Burcher heard their navigator, Ken Earnshaw, talking the pilot down to 60 feet on the intercom and then heard "Bomb gone" from the bomb aimer, John Fraser. Just at that moment there was a terrific crash and Burcher saw flames streaming past his turret on the port side. The flight engineer announced that the port outer engine was on fire. Burcher tried to rotate his turret but nothing happened. Hopgood feathered the port outer and called up the crew to discover the wireless operator had been badly hit in the leg and that there was still no answer from the front turret. With the port wing now ablaze Hopgood made a gallant attempt to gain height so that his crew could bale out and ordered them to do so. Burcher later said that Hopgood sounded totally calm and at ease just like he always did and as if nothing was wrong.

To get out of his turret which would not turn hydraulically because of the loss of hydraulic power, Burcher had to hand-crank the turret slowly round to the fore and aft position in order to vacate it and reach his parachute stowed in the fuselage. The aircraft was now vibrating badly in a gentle climbing starboard turn with both port engines knocked out. AJ-M's bomb had meanwhile bounced over the dam wall and completely destroyed the power house below. Inside the blazing Lancaster, the severely wounded wireless operator, Sergeant John Minchin, crawled towards Burcher who assisted him with his parachute and pushed him out into the darkness, pulling the D-ring release as he did so (sadly Minchin did not survive). Burcher then pulled his own parachute release while still in the aircraft. He knew it was not in the text books, but at this height he felt it was his only chance. Bundling his parachute under his arm, Burcher plugged in to the intercom by the rear door and informed the captain that he was baling out. Hopgood, who had managed to climb the aircraft to about 500 feet shouted: "For Christ's sake get out!" At that moment there was a terrific bang and a great rush of air. The flames had reached the main wing fuel tank which exploded. Burcher was blown out and smashed into the tailplane so violently that he cracked his spine. He

landed in the middle of a newly ploughed field which helped to cushion his fall from such a low height, but he broke his kneecap. He later said: "If John (Hopgood) had flown the Lancaster straight ahead, I would have landed in the path of the flood waters, and would almost definitely have drowned in them. Everything was on my side that night. I just wish it had been on the side of all of my crew. John Hopgood and Charlie Brennan had to know they were never going to escape from the aircraft in that kind of a situation and still give the aircrew a chance to get out. So they stayed to the end and I am alive because of it."

After the raid, Burcher was posted missing along with the rest of Hopgood's crew. He spent 12 months in German hospitals receiving treatment for his injuries. His survival as a prisoner of war was eventually communicated to the RAAF by his WAAF fianceé to whom he sent a Prisoner of War card from Stalag Luft III at Sagan, saying: "I have quite recovered and am being well treated. Unfortunately the rest of the crew were killed and so far it seems I am the only survivor... please write to the next-of-kin of the other members of the crew telling that the boys had a decent burial." (In fact, as we know, the bomb aimer, John Fraser, also survived and became a prisoner of war after being captured close to the Dutch border 10 days later). The card from Tony Burcher was the first confirmation that his fianceé received that he was in fact alive.

Burcher was liberated by the advancing Allies in May 1945 and returned to Australia in January 1946 having married his WAAF fianceé, Joan. He continued to serve with the RAAF until he transferred to the RAF as a flight lieutenant in 1952. He then saw further active service in Korea and Malaya with 205 Squadron on Short Sunderlands. He subsequently served with the same unit in Borneo in 1955 and with 209 Squadron in Malaya, eventually retiring with the rank of squadron leader.

Burcher was one of the 56 men who did not return home for Operation Chastise and he was one of only three of those who survived as POWs. He died of natural causes some years ago, having lived a full life. When asked in an interview before his death if he had any regrets, he said: "No, none whatsoever; I'd live it all again, and that includes the fact that I was shot down. I do regret, of course, that my mates were killed but I have no regrets for myself, I'd gladly live through it all again."

Top: Pilot Officer Tony Burcher DFM RAAF.

Above: Flt Lt John 'Hoppy' Hopgood, Burcher's pilot and the "bravest of the brave". (Author's Collection)

Medals

AWARDED TO THE DAMS RAID AIRCREW

Thirty four of the Dams Raid aircrew were decorated for their part in Operation Chastise, with the honours list first being published in the newspapers on May 28, 1943, along with detailed accounts of the visit to 617 Squadron at Scampton by King George VI and Queen Elizabeth, the day before. With the exception of one aircrew member, who was sick, the other 33 received their medals at an investiture at Buckingham Palace on the morning of June 22 from the queen, as the king was away in the Middle East. One of the squadron aircrew joked that it was necessary for the queen to carry out the investiture because there was no guarantee that "this lot will still be around when the king gets back".

Contrary to convention, the 'Dambusters' as they were now beginning to be called, were decorated together and they took precedence over all others waiting to be honoured. The airmen had travelled down to London from Grantham by train the day before the investiture, starting a serious drinking party and general hijinks on the train, which continued into the night in London. After the investiture the partying continued and that evening, joined by families and other members of the squadron, they attended a dinner hosted by A V Roe & Co at the Hungaria Restaurant in Lower Regent Street, London.

The reasoning behind the aircrew awards for the Dams Raid is not altogether clear and, as with most honours lists, seems somewhat unfair, with some worthy individuals left out. All the pilots, navigators and bomb aimers of the eight Lancasters that attacked the dams and returned were decorated. So were two wireless operators and six gunners (both gunners in Gibson's and Townsend's crews, and the rear gunners of Martin's and Shannon's crews). Only one flight engineer, Sergeant John Pulford of Gibson's crew, was decorated for the raid, all the others receiving no recognition for their actions.

The only complete crew to receive awards was Gibson's, while six of the seven men of Townsend's crew, the last to return, fighting their way out of enemy territory, were honoured. For some reason the flight engineer, Sergeant Powell, was the only one of Townsend's crew not decorated. Strangely, the crews of Squadron Leaders Young and Maudslay, and that of Flight Lieutenant Hopgood, which dropped their weapons against the dams, but were shot down and did not return home, did not receive any posthumous decorations, despite displaying great gallantry and paying the ultimate price.

Wing Commander Guy Gibson received the Victoria Cross (VC) for his leadership of the raid and also received the Bar to his DSO (which had been announced on March 30) at the same ceremony. As holder of the VC, DSO and Bar, DFC and Bar, he became the most decorated pilot in the RAF at that time. Flight Sergeant pilots Brown and Townsend received the rare and highly-regarded Conspicuous Gallantry Medal (CGM). Five Distinguished Service Orders (DSOs) were awarded, one each to Flight Lieutenants Martin, McCarthy, Maltby and Shannon, and one to Pilot Officer Knight, whose crew breached the Eder dam.

Fourteen Distinguished Flying Crosses (DFCs) and 12 Distinguished Flying Medals (DFMs) were awarded to the Dambuster aircrew. Flight Lieutenants Hay (bomb aimer on Martin's crew), Hutchison (wireless operator on Gibson's crew), Leggo (navigator on Martin's crew) and Walker (navigator on Shannon's crew) all received a Bar to their DFCs. Four of the commissioned navigators on crews that attacked the dams and returned – Flying Officers Hobday and Walker, and Pilot Officers Howard and Taerum – received DFCs. Similarly the NCO navigators on Maltby and Brown's crews – Sergeants Nicholson and Heal – were awarded the DFM. Apart from Gibson's wireless operator (Hutchison) only one other received a medal, Flight Sergeant Chalmers of Townsend's crew getting the DFM. As already mentioned, eight bomb aimers from those crews which dropped their weapons on target and returned were awarded DFCs or DFMs, according to their rank, while six of the 38 gunners who flew on the raid received DFCs or DFMs.

Throughout the text in this publication there is, inevitably, reference to the various medals mentioned above and held by individuals. For many not familiar with the British military honours system, the significance of these awards may not be clear and so a brief explanation of each follows:

VICTORIA CROSS

The Victoria Cross (VC) is quite simply the highest and most prestigious award for gallantry in the face of the enemy that can be awarded to British and Commonwealth forces. Originally instituted by Queen Victoria in 1856, it was intended as the highest possible decoration to attain, taking absolute precedence over all other awards and honours. The medal is awarded only for "most conspicuous bravery, a daring or pre-eminent act of valour, self-sacrifice or extreme devotion to duty in the presence of the enemy".

The medal is cast from bronze gunmetal supplied by the Royal Mint and always fashioned by the London firm of Messrs Hancock, which made the first Victoria Cross. The design, chosen by Queen Victoria, consists of a cross with the Royal Crest resting upon a scroll bearing the simple words: 'For Valour'. The reverse of the suspender bar is engraved with the recipient's name, rank and unit, while the reverse of the cross is engraved with the date of the deed for which the recipient was honoured. During the Second World War, 30 awards of the Victoria Cross were made to Allied airmen serving in the Royal Air Force and Royal Air Force Volunteer Reserve or the air forces of the Commonwealth countries.

DISTINGUISHED SERVICE ORDER

The Distinguished Service Order (DSO) was established in 1886 to reward officers who exhibited individual instances of meritorious or distinguished service in war.

It was usually awarded for service under fire or under conditions equivalent to service in actual combat with the enemy. However, during the First World War, from 1914 to 1916 it was awarded in some circumstances which could not be regarded as such, until January 1917, when commanders in the field were instructed to recommend the award of the DSO only for the original criteria. Prior to 1943, the order could be given only to someone who had already been 'mentioned in despatches'. The order is generally given to officers in command above the rank of major (squadron leader in the RAF) for "distinguished services during active operations against the enemy". Awards of the DSO to ranks below this are for a high degree of gallantry just short of deserving the Victoria Cross. It remains, however, an officers-only award and has never been awarded to a non-commissioned rank.

Above: (from left) Plt Off Spafford DFC DFM, Flt Lt Shannon DSO DFC, Flt Sgt Simpson DFM and Flt Lt Leggo DFC and Bar at the palace investiture. (Australian War Memorial UK0214)

The reasoning behind the aircrew awards is not altogether clear and seems somewhat unfair, with some worthy individuals left out.

DISTINGUISHED FLYING CROSS

The Distinguished Flying Cross (DFC) was instituted in 1919 by King George V. The DFC was to be awarded to British and Commonwealth officers of the RAF and other services for "an act or acts of valour, courage or devotion to duty while flying in active operations against the enemy". The decoration was initially intended to be awarded to commissioned officers and warrant officers. During the Second World War, some 20,354 DFCs were awarded (more than any other decoration of the war). In addition, there were 1550 first Bars (a second award of the same medal) and 46 second Bars. Since 1993, the DFC has been available to other ranks below commissioned officers and warrant officers.

DISTINGUISHED FLYING MEDAL

The Distinguished Flying Medal (DFM) was instituted in 1919 at the same time as the DFC. Like the DFC it was for "an act or acts of valour, courage or devotion to duty while flying in active operations against the

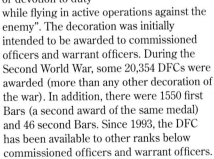

enemy", but the DFM was awarded only to non-commissioned ranks, rather than officers. During the Second World War 6637 DFMs were awarded, along with 60 first Bars. Only one person received a second Bar to the DFM – Flight Sergeant Don Kingaby in November 1944. With the reorganisation of the honours system in 1993, the DFM was discontinued.

CONSPICUOUS GALLANTRY MEDAL

The Conspicuous Gallantry Medal (CGM) was originally established by Queen Victoria in 1855, at the time of the Crimean War, as an award for bravery for Petty Officers and seamen of the Royal navy and non-commissioned officers (NCOs) and privates of the Royal Marines.

In November 1942, King George VI extended availability of the CGM to British and Commonwealth warrant officers and airmen for "acts of conspicuous gallantry whilst flying in active operations against the enemy". The decoration is second only to the VC and its award for services in the air is extremely rare with only a little over 100 being presented up until the reorganisation of the honours system in 1993, when it was discontinued.

'DAMBUSTER' GUNNER
FLIGHT SERGEANT FRED 'DOC' SUTHERLAND

Above: Les Knight's crew (from left) Harry Hobday, Edward Johnson, Fred Sutherland, Les Knight, Bob Kellow, Harry 'Obie' O'Brien and Ray Grayston.
(© IWM CH11049)

"Most of the time I can put it out of my mind and not think about it, but if I have to recall, I always lose some sleep."

Seventy-five years on from Operation Chastise, there are hardly any of the original survivors of the Dams Raid still alive to tell us their stories first-hand. One of the last eyewitnesses to that remarkable feat of arms is Fred Sutherland, who lives in Canada. Fred was the front gunner in the Lancaster which breached the Eder Dam on the night of May 16-17, 1943.

For many years Fred has been reticent about his wartime experiences, saying about recalling those events: "For some reason I find it quite stressful. Most of the time I can put it out of my mind and not think about it, but if I have to try to recall, I always lose some sleep."

Fred was also initially reluctant, out of modesty, to contribute to the publication of the story of his own personal experiences. However, recognising the importance of commemorating his colleagues, especially those who paid the ultimate price, he generously agreed to give his full co-operation and help allow me to tell his amazing story and that of his crew...

AIR GUNNER

Fred Sutherland was born on February 26, 1923. He volunteered for the Royal Canadian Air Force (RCAF) when he turned 18, as he explains: "I joined the RCAF in July of 1941 and by the fall I was in a manning depot holding unit, waiting to go on a course. In January 1942 an air gunners' course came up; 15 people signed up and we were in England for spring 1942. We had a brand new A/G wing, but didn't know too much about anything. My hurry was that I thought the war would be over before we got there.

"We crewed up with Sergeant Pilot Les Knight in August 1942. Our rear gunner was Harry O'Brien, from Regina, Saskatchewan; his nickname was Obie. When we first met as a crew at No 1654 Heavy Conversion Unit (HCU) at Wigsley, we looked ourselves over and O'Brien said to me: 'Which turret do you want?' I said: 'The top turret,' and he replied 'That's good because I would prefer the rear.'

LES KNIGHT

Their pilot, Les Knight, an Australian, had interrupted his accountancy studies to volunteer for the Royal Australian Air Force (RAAF) in early 1941 when he was 20 years old. Fred Sutherland says of him: "Les was short but very muscular, strong in the shoulders and arms. He was a wonderful pilot. He didn't smoke or drink and he was an example to all of us. He was a good disciplinarian. He was very quiet, but if you were out of line he quietly told you that you'd better not do that again. So we didn't. We respected and admired him. He was just a wonderful person."

When the crew originally came together, Les Knight was not commissioned, but after he became an officer in December 1942, he continued to visit the

Sergeants' Mess regularly to make sure that the NCOs still felt part of the crew.

During their course at the HCU the crew suffered a flying accident, fortunately with no injuries, as Fred explains: "We started out with an engineer called Syd. One night we were doing circuits and bumps in a Manchester. While coming in for the 'bump' Syd was fooling around with the petrol cocks when he turned off the fuel supply to the engines, which stopped. The Manchester did not glide very far without power and we came very near to knocking off the ancient church that was in the glide path. The Manchester was written off.

On the way to see the CO, Syd said to Les: "We will have to get together on our story." Les was quite angry and he said in a few words: "What story? There is only one story." After the meeting with the CO we never saw Syd again. That was our first engineer. We had three engineers. The last one, Ray Grayston, was knowledgeable and courageous and he was a real asset to the crew. He died at his home in Woodhall Spa in 2010."

50 SQUADRON

In September 1942, the crew joined No 50 Squadron, which had recently replaced its Avro Manchesters with Lancasters. The squadron was based at RAF Swinderby, but moved to RAF Skellingthorpe in mid-October that year. By March 1943 the crew had completed 25 operational sorties. Fred Sutherland was still only just 20 years old. The two gunners, Fred and Obie, were two unattached youngsters and they gained a reputation for being rather wild, but they never reported unfit for duty. Fred says: "We did consume a lot of beer and we were always broke before payday. I think it was a case of having a few drinks to try to forget the future. On standby we were not allowed to drink, so we were always glad to see a few wet days."

617 SQUADRON

"One day towards the end of March 1943 we were called in as a crew and asked if we would be willing to join a new squadron being formed by Wing Commander Gibson. We could stay together as a crew and we would be credited with a full tour of 30 trips. We liked each other and we thought we could do another 20 ops and be done. We didn't want to start over again with a 'green' pilot and a brand new crew."

The crew, like others, had been chosen because of its bombing record. Fred clearly does not believe that they were doing anything particularly special by volunteering to join this new elite outfit – 617 Squadron as it was soon numbered – although they were, of course, volunteering for unknown duties and for additional operations beyond the 30 of a normal tour.

Several weeks of intensive training followed, to prepare the crews for ultra low-level flying and navigation at night. Fred remembers: "We flew a lot of 'cross-countries' up as far as Scotland and round the Lake District, just low level. I remember those canals in northern England and flying along those, and I think it was all navigation and map reading. Johnson (the bomb aimer) was the expert map reader and Hobday was a marvellous navigator; together they just made a real team."

The gunners practised their air-to-ground gunnery against a smoke float dropped in the Wash ranges, "shooting it up pretty good". The reason for all this training remained a mystery to the crews.

"We never did know what the target was until the day of the raid; most thought it was U-boat pens. So

Below: Gunners Fred Sutherland (left) and Harry O'Brien. (Author's Collection)

Bottom: A 617 Squadron Lancaster low flying training over England. (Author's Collection)

"We consumed a lot of beer and were always broke... It was a case of having a few drinks to forget the future."

far as I know no person guessed it was the dams. We were told not to guess and not to talk about anything to do with flying."

As for the amazing Barnes Wallis Upkeep bouncing bomb or mine, Ray Grayston, the flight engineer, later said: "When we first saw Upkeep, we were amazed at the idea that it would work at all. It horrified us to think they'd put this b***** great lump of metal, like a cricket pitch roller, underneath the Lancaster, which interfered with the handling of the aircraft."

THE DAMS RAID

On Sunday, May 16, 1943, the operation was declared ON. Fred remembers the lengthy briefing for all the aircrew flying on the mission, held at 1800 in the upstairs briefing room at Scampton, when the targets – the dams – were revealed. Barnes Wallis was present at this briefing and Fred particularly remembers Gibson's 'pep' talk when he told the assembled crews: "If you don't do it tonight, you're going back tomorrow night."

Les Knight and his crew took off from Scampton at 21:59 hours, as part of the first wave of nine aircraft, in Type 464 Lancaster ED912, coded AJ-N, carrying a 9000lb Upkeep bouncing bomb. With the mid-upper turret removed on these specially modified Lancasters, Fred Sutherland was operating the front turret in expectation of the need to suppress enemy ground fire, especially on the attack runs.

On reaching the first target, Knight and his crew orbited patiently while the lead crews went in to attack and eventually to successfully breach the Möhne Dam. Sadly, Flight Lieutenant John 'Hoppy' Hopgood's aircraft was shot down by ground fire during his attack on the Möhne, with five of the crew perishing and two miraculously surviving to be taken prisoner. If the risks of this venture had not been apparent to the crews before, they were now quite obvious. Wing Commander Guy Gibson then led the remaining three Lancasters of the first wave, including AJ-N 'Nuts', to the Eder, some 12 minutes' flying time away.

THE EDER DAM

The Eder Dam was undefended as the Germans had such confidence that its position and the surrounding

Above: The Eder (showing the surrounding hills and Waldeck Castle top right). (Author's Collection)

Below: Knight's crew's aircraft AJ-N. (Illustration by Chris Sandham-Bailey / INKWORM © 2010)

terrain, with hills up to over 1300ft in places and with a curved approach to the dam, made it effectively impregnable to attack from the air.

Flight Lieutenant Dave Shannon was ordered to make the first attack, but he had great difficulty achieving the correct height and approach on three attempts and was unable to achieve the correct drop parameters. Shannon later recalled: "The Eder was a bugger of a job. I was the first to go; I tried three times to get a spot-on approach but was never satisfied. To get out of the valley after crossing the dam wall we had to put on full throttle and do a steep climbing turn to avoid a vast rock face. My exit with a 9000lb bomb revolving at 500rpm was bloody hairy!"

Gibson then ordered Squadron Leader Henry Maudslay to make his run. Again, the crew struggled to find the correct height and direction on the first two attempts, so Shannon was brought in to try again and he finally released his Upkeep. The bomb bounced twice before exploding and, as the water settled, a slight breach was noticeable, but it was not sufficient to cause the dam to fail. Then Maudslay made another attempt, but he released his bomb too late. The mine bounced off the dam wall and exploded in mid-air right under the Lancaster, which was seriously damaged by the blast. Maudslay limped away from the scene, only to be shot down on the way home by light flak, with the loss of all the crew.

Finally, Les Knight was called in, with the last remaining Upkeep from the nine aircraft assigned to the Möhne and Eder Dams. From the nose turret, Fred Sutherland had a grandstand view of the immensely difficult attack run and the exit from the target, and a free 'fairground ride' to boot!

It started with a steep dive from 1000 feet, pointing towards a point on the promontory in front of the dam, with the prominent Waldeck Castle, on its knoll, immediately to their left. During this steep dive, the engines were set at high rpm and the flaps were set to 10 degrees, to help in controlling the speed.

Levelling off sharply at very low level over the water, the aircraft then had to be flung into a hard left turn, then it had to be 'hopped' over the spit before quickly settling down at 60 feet and lined up with the dam. There were only about five to seven seconds to get settled at the correct height, to line up with the target and to release the bomb at the correct range

before it was too late. After crossing the dam, the aircraft had to "stand on its tail" with full emergency power to clear the high ground ahead. All this, of course, in the dark!

Fred was just a passenger during the attack runs. He was aware of "quite a vibration" through the aircraft as the Upkeep revolved beneath it and especially when it was released. In the subsequent climb to clear the large hill facing the dam, both the bomb aimer (Edward Johnson) and Fred in the nose of the aircraft got a hair-raising and much-too-close-for-comfort view of the approaching rock face. Fred says that it was "pretty scary, as we came close to the top of the hill".

Fred describes the crew co-operation required and the crew's total confidence in their pilot thus: "There were five main players in the dropping of the spinning bomb. First the pilot, Les Knight; we all had the utmost confidence in his skills and his quick grasp of

Above: 'Breaching the Eder Dam' by Robert Taylor. As Les Knight's Lancaster AJ-N climbs away, its Upkeep explodes against the Eder Dam, breaching it. (© The Military Gallery, Wendover, UK)

a problem in an emergency. He was very quiet but quick to act without panic when action was required.

"Then there was the bomb aimer, the navigator, the engineer and the radio operator. Each of these people had an important job to perform to make the dropping of the bouncing bomb a success.

"Here we are flying down into the steep valley where the Eder Dam is located. The engineer is responsible for correct air speed. He is calling out the air speed over the intercom. The navigator is trying to get the correct height from the spotlights; he is telling the pilot "up" or "down" or "steady" while the bomb aimer is saying "left, left" or "right, right" and the wireless op is reporting revs of the bomb. When the bomb aimer said "bomb gone", we went into a steep climb with the throttles pushed through the 'gate'. Everything worked perfectly (I have always been thankful to the ground crew for their expert maintenance). All this is taking place in less than 1½ miles at 230mph – very few seconds to do the job. At the time I didn't appreciate the skill and the luck involved, but I was very proud to be part of that particular crew."

After one aborted 'dummy run' and with some brilliant flying and some excellent crew co-operation, the Les Knight crew released their Upkeep perfectly on the second run. The mine bounced three times before striking the dam slightly to the right of centre. In the ensuing explosion, the dam was seen to shake visibly before the already weakened masonry began to crumble and a massive breach appeared. O'Brien, the rear gunner, called on the intercom: "It's gone!" as he got a grandstand view of a large gap appearing in the dam wall and water gushing from it. Knight circled back over the dam and Fred marvelled at "the unbelievable force of the water coming out and how high it was".

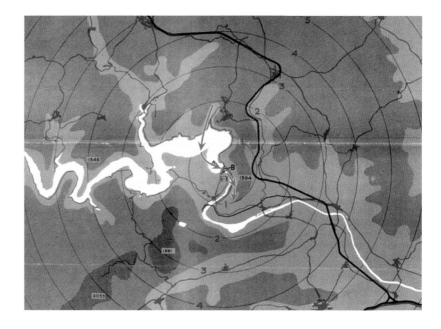

The RAF target map of the Eder, with the immensely difficult attack route superimposed. (Crown Copyright)

The breached Eder Dam, the morning after the raid. (© PA Images)

After landing safely back at Scampton at 04:20 hours, the tired crew were elated that they had survived and at their success; but when the true extent of the squadron's losses became apparent (40% of the aircrew on the mission were killed) they were deeply saddened. Les Knight was subsequently awarded the DSO for his part in the raid, while the navigator, Flying Officer 'Harry' Hobday, and the bomb aimer, Flying Officer Edward Johnson, were awarded immediate DFCs.

The other four members of the crew, all NCOs, were pleased for their commissioned colleagues but they themselves went unrewarded.

AFTER THE DAMS RAID

Over the next several weeks 617 Squadron was rebuilt with replacement aircraft and crews. While Bomber Command sought to find a role for this specialist low-level bombing unit, it was tasked on three nights in July with attacking long-range targets in Italy, so-called shuttle raids, where the force flew on to North Africa to refuel and rearm before returning a few days later, usually bombing a different target on the way back.

Fred Sutherland's crew were sent on a 'Nickel' raid dropping leaflets on Milan on July 29, landing at Blida in North Africa and returning home on August 1. Neither they nor the rest of the squadron were impressed that they were being used to drop leaflets. Wing Commander Guy Gibson was posted out on August 3 and replaced as CO by Squadron Leader George Holden, who was soon promoted to wing commander. On August 30, 1943, No 617 Squadron moved to RAF Coningsby (the airfield that, by a quirk of fate, is now home to the BBMF Lancaster). On September 12, the 617 Squadron operational records book recorded Fred Sutherland's promotion to flight sergeant.

THE DORTMUND-EMS CANAL RAID – SEPTEMBER 1943

The next special mission for the squadron was a low-level raid, using the new 12,000-lb High Capacity (HC), thin-case, 'blockbuster' blast bomb – the biggest bomb the RAF had yet carried – in an attempt to breach the Dortmund-Ems canal, a vital artery of the German transport system.

The 168 mile-long canal linked the Ruhr valley to the sea; it carried millions of tons of freight each year and was crucial to the German economy and war effort.

At Ladbergen, just south of the junction with the Mittelland Canal, there is a raised section where aqueducts carry the canal over a river. This had long been a target that the RAF was keen to attack, but which, so far, it had failed to breach. Now it had a new weapon, three times the size of the normal 4000lb 'cookie'. The plan was to drop these from very low height into the soft earth embankments of the raised waterways. A delayed fuse would give the Lancasters time to get away before the huge explosion. A direct hit would not only breach the canal wall, emptying the canal, but would also flood the surrounding countryside.

The operation turned into a disaster from the first night. Eight Lancasters set off from Coningsby in the late evening of September 14, 1943, but the mission was aborted when poor weather conditions over the target were reported by a reconnaissance Mosquito. The recall signal from the operations room at No 5 Group HQ was received by the Lancaster formation when they were an hour out, flying at very low level over the North Sea. As the bombers turned around to head for home, somehow David Maltby's Lancaster hit the sea. All the crew were lost.

The next night they went again with eight aircraft in two flights of four aircraft each. Flight Lieutenant Les Knight and his crew were in Lancaster B1 JB144, KC-N, with Fred Sutherland in the front turret. Unusually, each Lancaster had a crew of eight, with three gunners per aircraft so that the front, mid-upper and rear turrets were continuously manned for this low level operation.

Fred describes the crew's reaction to their new, additional crew member: "On the night of the Dortmund disaster we had a third gunner by the

Above: RAF photo-reconnaissance image of the breached Eder dam, taken the morning after Operation Chastise.
(Crown Copyright)

Above: Hobday, Knight and Johnson after their palace investiture.
(Author's Collection)

name of Sergeant Les Woollard. The first time we ever saw him was the first night, when he was brought out to the aircraft. He had obviously had some experience because one of the first things he did for good luck was to go and have a pee on the tail wheel! We rushed to stop him, but too late, it was done. We were not superstitious but we always did the same routine. I always ate my chocolate bar when we were charging down the runway, and I always wore the same socks that my girlfriend, now my wife, had knitted for me." Woollard's actions had clearly compromised the crew's normal routine and this was not a good omen.

After crossing into Germany, the lead aircraft, flown by Wing Commander Holden, was hit by flak in the starboard wing. It caught fire, crashed and exploded; all the crew were killed instantly.

As the remaining Lancasters approached the target area, a heavy mist appeared which obscured the ground and made ultra low-level formation flying impossible. The crews spent nearly an hour searching individually for the target in the fog, at low level. Three more were shot down by flak and, while trying to find the target, Les Knight's aircraft, with Fred in the front turret, hit some trees on a small ridge. It staggered away with both port engines failing due to tree-damaged radiators and with a seriously damaged tail.

> "If we were caught we would go to prison camp; if they were caught, they were dead along with their families."

Despite the immediate danger, Les Knight sought permission from the leader to jettison his bomb and this was granted. The crew also threw out guns, ammunition and anything else that they could to save weight, which allowed Les to coax the aircraft up to almost 1400 feet. The damage was causing the aircraft to want to turn continuously to the left and Les Knight was using full opposite controls and all his strength to try to keep the wings level. Shortly, one of the two remaining starboard engines also failed.

Knight ordered the crew to bail out, knowing that he, himself, had little chance of surviving. Fred Sutherland and Les Woollard were down the back of the Lancaster, where they had been trying to lighten the load by throwing things out of the door. Fred says:

"Woollard and I baled out of the side door and I never saw him again." Ray Grayston, the flight engineer, was the last to leave, saying a final farewell to his captain, who was struggling heroically with the controls to maintain height for long enough for his crew to escape. Shortly afterwards the aircraft hit the ground with Les Knight still on board and he was killed. He was subsequently buried in the cemetery at Den Ham, in the Netherlands.

Adding to the tragedy and the sense of pointless loss of lives, the mission was a total failure; no damage was done to the canal. Only three of the eight Lancasters returned safely to Coningsby; the other five were shot down or crashed. A total of 33 men lost their lives in this disaster; probably the blackest hour in the history of 617 Squadron. Fred Sutherland's view of this disaster and the impact on him is typically understated: "The Dortmund Canal raid was a disaster from the first night when we lost Dave Maltby. The second night was worse when we lost five experienced crews. One can't lay blame, but, several costly mistakes were made."

EVADING

Of the seven members of Les Knight's crew who baled out, all survived. Two of them, Ray Grayston (the flight engineer) and Harry O'Brien (the rear gunner) were captured and spent the rest of the war as POWs; amazingly, the other five evaded capture. Over the next 10 weeks, with the help of the Dutch, Belgian and French Resistance movements and Basque guides, four of the crew, including Fred Sutherland, made their way to Gibraltar via the Pyrenees and from there to England.

Fred says: "Johnson was the most prepared to escape. For these low level jobs he always wore walking shoes and clothes that could be worn under his battle dress. I think he made more miles than any of us before he got help. Bob Kellow was the other of our crew who made a lot of miles on his own before getting help." Sergeant Woollard also evaded capture and, helped by the Underground movements, eventually made his way back to England by boat from Brittany in January 1944. Woollard was a married man whose wife was expecting their first child; he was home in time to be present at the birth. Fred believes that five crew members evading successfully from a single crew is something of a record.

The detail of Fred's 'home run' would make an epic story in its own right. He has given us some glimpses of his experiences 'on the run' and clearly has deep feelings of gratitude towards those who helped him and his colleagues: "This was at a time when the Germans had infiltrated the Underground and the whole organisation had broken down. They did not know who they could trust. The people who helped us did so at a tremendous risk to themselves and their families. If we were caught we would likely go to prison camp; if they were caught, they were dead along with their families.

"I cannot say enough about the people who helped me. People took us into their homes and fed us, although we were complete strangers. We stayed with a Dutch policeman who was in charge of a political jail at Scheveningen. He was later caught by the Germans and was sentenced to death three times; somehow he survived and was eventually liberated by the US Army. He came out blind and weighed 80 pounds. He emigrated to Canada and lived for several years; but from his treatment his heart was in poor condition and he died quite young.

"When Hobday and I were in Rotterdam we watched Henk Lindeman forge a travel paper on stolen stationery. The next night we had to hand the papers to a German officer who was checking documents at the border between Belgium and France. He held mine up to the light for a better look before handing it back. That was my worst experience; or the one I remember most vividly.

"Hobday and I also stayed with a 65-year-old lady in Paris for a month. She fed us and kept us in her apartment with Germans in the same building. I am at a loss to describe the kind of courage these people have. I am grateful and I will admire them as long as I am here.

"After Gibraltar we flew back to England in a Liberator. Hobday and I were interviewed by MI9 in Gib and then the same procedure in London. We were not allowed to talk to anyone; Hobday was not allowed to see his wife till the interview was over. We were not to tell who our helpers were or where they lived."

The great majority of successful evaders at that time were not allowed to return to 'ops' for fear of further capture and the subsequent risk to the safety of the gallant resistance workers and 'helpers' on the Continent. Fred was posted back to Canada and became a gunnery instructor on the West Coast in B-24 Liberators and B-25 Mitchells. After a year he was discharged from the RCAF and went back to school. He worked his way to university and gained a degree in forestry.

POST WAR

After the war ended Fred worked for the British Columbia and the Alberta Forest Services. On occasions, when there were multiple forest fires and there was a shortage of forestry staff, Fred volunteered to fly as an observer in firefighting aircraft. On one such flight in the 1970s his aircraft crashed in the mountains.

He described the event thus: "The visibility was very poor because of fires in British Columbia. When we got into the mountains I think we could see less than a mile. We turned into the wrong valley and could not climb out of it – not enough power – the pilot tried to turn but we were losing altitude and the stall warning was going. We hit the rocks, knocked the port wing off and burst into flames; luckily the fire did not last long." The crew was all rescued by helicopter – Fred's luck had held again!

Despite the enormous risks of the wartime missions that Fred and his crew were involved in with the Dambusters, Fred believes that those who joined 617 Squadron later were the brave ones. He says: "There was some wonderful work done later by 617 Squadron, often accompanied by 9 Squadron. The point I am trying to make is that those people joined the squadron knowing its reputation. These men had real courage and deserve a lot of credit."

This is a typically self-deprecating remark from a very modest man whose own courage is obvious and not in doubt. I am very grateful to Fred Sutherland for allowing me to tell his story, with his help, which gives a different perspective on the well-known story of the Dams Raid, which has subsequently become a legend.

Above: 12,000lb HC bomb in front of Les Knight's Lancaster B1 JB144 KC-N.
(Crown Copyright)
Above: Plt Off Les Knight DSO (RAAF).
(Author's Collection)
Above left: Fred now, at home in Canada.
(courtesy Fred Sutherland)

"I'm at a loss to describe the courage these people have. I am grateful and I will admire them as long as I am here."

Dambuster formation (then and now). RAF BBMF Lancaster PA474, wearing the colour scheme of Thumper Mk.III which flew with 617 Squadron from late 1943 until the end of the Second World War. A Tornado GR4 – the current equipment of 617 Squadron – flies alongside the old bomber. In recent times the 617 Squadron Tornados and their crews have been actively involved in operations in Iraq and Afghanistan. (© Richard Paver 2012)

Beyond the dams
617 SQUADRON DURING THE REST OF THE WAR

After Operation Chastise, Air Chief Marshal Sir Arthur Harris – the Commander-in-Chief of Bomber Command – decided that, despite his instinctive mistrust and dislike of elite units, 617 Squadron would be retained as a specialist, precision-bombing unit.

On June 3, 1943, he announced: "It is my intention to keep the squadron for the performance of similar tasks in the future." Although exactly what these tasks might be was yet to be decided.

Those with some knowledge of the history of 617 Squadron are aware of the important and demanding operations completed by the unit during the remainder of the war, and of the great skill and courage shown by the crews. However, for many, the exploits of the original Dambusters on Operation Chastise overshadow the actions of those who followed and there is less awareness of what 617 Squadron achieved during the latter stages of the war in Europe. This is a shame, because, as Fred Sutherland, one of the few surviving original Dambusters, said to me: "Those who joined 617 Squadron later on were the brave ones. There was some wonderful work done later by 617 Squadron... these men had real courage and deserve a lot of credit."

After the losses of the Dams Raid, new crews were posted in as replacements and the squadron also received replacement Lancasters of the standard type (BIs and BIIIs). The squadron returned to operations on July 24 and 25, 1943, with a so-called 'shuttle' raid on targets in Italy, then landing in Africa to refuel and re-arm, and attacking another target on the return flight to England. Two power stations in northern Italy were successfully attacked on the way out and the target for the return trip was the docks at Leghorn, Italy. On August 3, 1943, Squadron Leader George Holden

DSO DFC and Bar became the new Commanding Officer (CO) of 617 Squadron when Guy Gibson was posted away.

THE DORTMUND-EMS DISASTER

In August 1943, the airfield at RAF Scampton, which had been home to 617 Squadron since its formation in March that year, was closed so that hard runways could be built on the grass airfield. The squadron moved to Coningsby and it was from here that the ill-fated Dortmund-Ems canal raid was launched in September 1943. This raid has already been covered in some detail in the earlier chapter 'Dambuster Gunner', but in many ways it was the squadron's darkest hour. Across two nights (bad weather caused the operation to be aborted on the first night September 14), it cost the lives of 41 men (there were eight in each crew, with three gunners per aircraft, for this operation), including 12 of the original surviving Dambusters. The commanding officer, Wing Commander Holden, was one of those killed. Apart from those who lost their lives, seven airmen baled out of Les Knight's aircraft over enemy territory; two became POWs and five were on the run. Only three of the eight Lancasters which set out from Coningsby on the night of September 15-16 returned home.

Other crews in Bomber Command, who knew of the percentage losses suffered by 617 Squadron both on Operation Chastise and then on their next major operation against the Dortmund-Ems canal, must have thought that it was almost a 'suicide outfit'. Yet experienced bomber aircrew due for rest tours still volunteered to join the elite unit. Despite their losses on the night of September 15-16, 617 Squadron was on ops again the following night, when six aircraft were sent to bomb the Antheor Viaduct on the French-Italian border, unfortunately without success.

Above: The RAF Battle of Britain Memorial Flight Lancaster B1 PA474 in the colours of 617 Sqn Lancaster DV385, KC-A Thumper Mk.III. (Crown Copyright 2012)

BLOCKBUSTER

The weapon used on the Dortmund-Ems canal raid – the 12,000lb (5448kg) HC (High Capacity) blockbuster bomb – was the second special weapon employed by 617 Squadron since its formation and confirmed the squadron as a specialist unit. This was the biggest bomb that the RAF had so far used and was created by bolting together three sections of the standard 4000lb blast-bomb – the so-called 'cookie' – used by Bomber Command Main Force aircraft. This bomb could only be carried in specially modified Lancasters, with bulged or 'blown' bomb bay doors enlarged to fit around the big bomb, which were delivered to 617 Squadron from September 1943. The 12,000lb HC bomb became 617 Squadron's distinctive weapon until the deep penetration Tallboy earthquake bombs became available some nine months later.

THE CHESHIRE ERA

Wing Commander Leonard Cheshire, already the holder of the DSO and two Bars and the DFC, arrived as commanding officer of 617 Squadron in November 1943 and so began the squadron's highly successful 'Cheshire era'. On January 9, 1944, the squadron moved the few miles north to RAF Woodhall Spa, which was to be the unit's base for the rest of the war. Work on building the airfield at Woodhall Spa had begun in 1941, the site was originally wooded and some of the woodland had been retained in the northeastern part of the airfield, providing good cover for some of the more secretive aspects of 617's operations, including the bomb store. In Woodhall Spa village, the large and impressive building that is now the Petwood Hotel and which had been the country home of Sir Archibald and Lady Weigall, was requisitioned by the RAF as the Officers' Mess and became the home for the squadron's officers.

During the Cheshire era, 617 Squadron emerged from being a unit which had performed one incredible mission, to being, indisputably, the elite squadron in Bomber Command. Some of the most important of the squadron's precision bombing missions are covered in the chapter which follows about one of its Lancasters during the period from December 1943 to the end of the war – DV385, Thumper Mk.III. This also details the amazing Barnes Wallis designed Tallboy deep penetration earthquake bomb and the special bombsight – the Stabilising Automatic Bomb Sight (SABS) Mk.IIA – which 617 Squadron used to achieve the necessary accuracy and which permitted true precision bombing from medium altitude for the first time in the RAF's history.

Above: Leonard Cheshire became OC 617 Sqn in November 1943. (© IWM CH 12667)

TARGET MARKING

Precision bombing of this sort required very accurate marking of the targets and Leonard Cheshire developed new marking techniques, initially employing low-level dive-bombing tactics with Lancasters. This was first tried operationally on February 8, 1944, against the Gnome-Rhone aero-engine factory at Limoges, when Cheshire flew three low-level passes over the factory to warn the French workers and then dropped his markers from 50 feet right in the centre of the target! The target was severely damaged by the subsequent bombing. From here on, the squadron marked its own targets, removing the need for Pathfinder force aircraft to support them, and the consistent accuracy of their marking and bombing not only proved extremely effective, but also significantly reduced collateral damage.

The Lancaster was not ideally suited to Cheshire's low-level, dive-bombing, marking techniques and he persuaded the Air Officer Commanding 5 Group to allow him to use the faster and more agile DH Mosquito for the task. After trying out a night fighter Mosquito at RAF Coleby Grange (not far from 617's home at Woodhall Spa) Cheshire flew the first such operation on April 5, 1944, in borrowed Mosquito ML976. He successfully marked the aircraft repair facility at Toulouse in France, for Lancasters of

617 emerged from being a unit which performed one incredible mission, to being the elite of Bomber Command

Left: Cheshire's flares, dropped from 50ft, explode on the Gnome-Rhone aero-engine factory. (© IWM 93014)

5 Group to bomb. Subsequently, four 617 Squadron crews were specially trained and Mosquitos were used for marking targets very successfully by the squadron until October 1944, after which time all low-level marking for all of 5 Group, including 617 Squadron, was done by 627 Squadron. This unit was co-located with 617 at Woodhall Spa and, from April 1944, lent various Mosquitos to 617 Squadron for their operations until two 'Mossies' were issued to the squadron. Even after that, 617 borrowed Mosquitos from 627 whenever it was necessary. The two Mosquitos on the strength of 617 Squadron have become near-mythical, with few photographs of them in existence and none that show what squadron markings, if any, they carried. The 617 Squadron Official Record Book (ORB) shows that the Mosquitos used most frequently on operations by the squadron were FB Mk.VIs NS993 (which was often flown by Cheshire and later by his successor Wing Commander Tait) and NT205, which flew the most ops. Mosquito FB VI NT202 may also have been on the strength of the squadron rather than being a borrowed aircraft, possibly replacing NS993.

The two Mosquitos on the strength of 617 have become near-mythical, with few photographs of them in existence.

From June 1944, Cheshire (and later Tait) sometimes used a P-51 Mustang III, HB837, for marking targets. Legend has it that the first night operation that Cheshire flew in the single-seat, single-engine fighter aircraft, against the V-weapon storage site at Siracourt on June 25, 1944, was his first sortie on type.

D-DAY AND AFTER

The special 'spoof' operation – Operation Taxable – conducted by 617 Squadron on June 5, 1944, the night before D-day, is mentioned in the story of Thumper Mk.III, which was one of the aircraft which participated. This operation does not, perhaps, always get the credit it deserves. It could be considered one of the most important carried out by 617, even though there was no visual effect and no bombs were dropped. The 'window' (chaff, to use modern parlance) corridor that was sown by the squadron's aircraft convinced the Germans that a fleet of ships was moving toward the Pas de Calais at eight knots, while the real D-Day armada headed for the Normandy beaches. Creating this illusion on the German radar screens required meticulous flying, navigation and timing, as an error of only four seconds could have made the 'ghost convoy' look suspect.

Two days after D-Day, on June 8, 1944, 617 Squadron dropped the first Tallboys against the

Saumur railway tunnel and the Tallboy then became the squadron's weapon of choice, mainly for targeting V-weapon sites and U-boat or E-boat pens. On June 14, the squadron flew its first daylight operations to drop Tallboys on the E-boat pens at Le Havre. More daylight operations were to follow, many of them part of the campaign against the German V-weapon sites.

In July 1944, Cheshire was posted from the squadron, having flown a total of 100 operations. His flight commanders, Squadron Leaders Dave Shannon, Les Munro and Joe McCarthy – all original Dambusters – were also rested. Cheshire's replacement as commanding officer was the youthful-looking, 26-year-old Wing Commander J B 'Willie' Tait DSO and Bar, DFC (Tait received a second bar to his DSO in September 1944).

TIRPITZ

Operations continued as before under Tait, mostly daylight Tallboy-dropping missions. On September 11, 1944, the squadron undertook the first of three operations, all of which were led by Tait, against the pocket battleship Tirpitz, moored in Kaa Fjord in northern Norway. A force of 38 Lancasters of 9 and 617 Squadrons (9 Squadron was the only other Tallboy capable unit in the RAF) set out to fly to an airfield in Northern Russia which was to be used as a base for an attack on the battleship. Several of the bombers were forced to crash-land and only 27 took off on September 15, 20 of them carrying Tallboys. With mountains screening the Lancasters' approach from enemy radar, the Tirpitz was caught by surprise and her smoke screens were late to start. One Tallboy smashed through the Tirpitz's forecastle and burst deep in her hull. The shock caused by the explosion of this bomb, or possibly other bombs which were near misses, also damaged the ship's engines. All of the Lancasters returned safely to Russia and subsequently flew back to the UK.

The Germans decided that it was not practical to make Tirpitz fully seaworthy again and she was moved to Tromso, further south in Norway, but only for use as a semi-static, heavy artillery battery. The British were not aware of the extent of the damage to the ship and Tromso Fjord was just in range of specially modified Lancasters flying out and back from Britain. With the removal of the Lancaster's mid-upper gun turrets and the installation of extra fuel tanks, the Tirpitz could be attacked from northern Scotland, although it required a 2250 mile round trip. Thirty-seven modified Lancasters were duly dispatched from Lossiemouth, Scotland, against the Tirpitz on October 29. The weather was ideal for the attack until an unexpected wind shift covered the battleship with cloud just 30 seconds before the first Lancaster was ready to bomb. Thirty-two aircraft released Tallboys on the estimated position but no direct hits were scored. The Germans responded by basing a fighter wing at a nearby airfield.

The third and final attack against the Tirpitz took place on November 12, 1944. Thirty Lancasters from 9 Squadron and 617 Squadron, led by Willie Tait, set off from Lossiemouth again. The weather was clear as

Below: 'Willie' Tait (fifth from left) and crew after returning from sinking the Tirpitz on November 12, 1944. Note the lack of the mid-upper turret. (© IWM CH 17864)

With mountains screening the Lancasters' approach from enemy radar, the Tirpitz was caught by surprise.

Below: The 'pocket battleship' Tirpitz. (Author's Collection)

the bombers flew at 1000 feet to avoid early detection by enemy radar, prior to rendezvousing at a lake 100 miles southeast of Tromso. The attacking force then climbed to bombing height – between 12,000 and 16,000 feet – and the warship was sighted from about 20 miles away. For some reason, despite frantic calls for air cover to the German fighter base at Bardufoss, not a single Luftwaffe fighter seems to have taken off. There was no smoke screen as the Lancasters passed over the last mountain and the fjord as the Tirpitz came into view. When the bombers were about 13 miles away, the anti-aircraft guns of the Tirpitz opened fire and were then joined by shore batteries and two flak ships. The first Tallboys narrowly missed the target, but then the Tirpitz was hit by three bombs. A column of steam and smoke shot up to about 300 feet and within a few minutes the ship had started to list badly. It then suffered a tremendous explosion as the ammunition stores magazine went up; the great ship rolled over to port and started to capsize. About 10 minutes after the first bomb had struck, the Tirpitz had completely turned turtle with only the hull visible. Around 1000 of her crew were killed. None of the attacking aircraft were significantly damaged and all returned safely to base. The Tirpitz had survived 33 previous attacks over three years, but not this one.

On December 28, 1944, 617 Squadron got its fourth commanding officer since its formation, when Willie Tait was replaced by Group Captain 'Johnny' Fauquier DSO and Bar DFC, an older and highly experienced Canadian pilot who took a drop in rank from Air Commodore so that he could take command of the squadron. Tait was awarded a third Bar to his

Above: Lancaster B1 (Special) PD114 YZ-B, over Arbergen on March 21, 1943. (© IWM C5102)
Below: Reconnaissance of the capsized Tirpitz. (Crown Copyright)
Bottom: Lancaster B1 (Special) with a Grand Slam. (© IWM MH4263)

DSO (he already had a Bar to his DFC), which was a record and many believe that he was close to receiving a VC. He had flown 101 bombing missions during the war. Johnny Fauquier was a good choice as the new CO of the elite unit; he was an exacting commander and ensured that 617 crews did not get above themselves at this late stage of the war.

GRAND SLAM

The spring of 1945 saw 617 Squadron armed with its fourth special weapon of the war when Grand Slam, the big brother of Tallboy, came into use in March. Grand Slam was huge: over 25 feet long and weighing 21,500lb (10 tons or 9752kg). The great size and weight of the new bomb required a specially modified variant of the Lancaster – the BI (Special) – to carry it. This version of the Lancaster had the bomb bay doors removed (harking back to the squadron's first specially modified Type 464 aircraft used on the Dams Raid) and the massive bomb was carried semi-recessed beneath the aircraft. To save weight, both the front and mid-upper gun turrets were removed on the B1 (Special). The wireless operator's station was also removed and the standard crew was only five men. The undercarriage of these aircraft was strengthened and they were even fitted with different, ribbed tyres. The first operational use of Grand Slam was on March 14, 1945, when one was dropped from BI (Special), PD112, YZ-S by Squadron leader 'Jock'

Calder and his crew, against the Bielefeld viaduct, along with a dozen Tallboys from other 617 Squadron aircraft. The big bomb brought down five arches on both sides of the double viaduct. It is estimated that, prior to this, more than 3000 tons of bombs had been dropped against the viaduct without success. Only 42 Grand Slams were dropped in the final two months of the war in Europe, all by 617 Squadron. The Tallboy and Grand Slam, together with the precision skills and SABs equipment of 617 Squadron, enabled the destruction of hardened targets that no other bombs could even damage, and allowed the RAF to attack pinpoint targets.

DANGER AND DEATH TO THE END

The German fighter force was largely spent by this stage of the war and gave the 617 Lancasters few problems, but the enemy flak remained a very dangerous threat on the daylight raids that were now the 'norm', especially as the SABS bombsight required a long straight run-in to the target. On March 21, 1945, during a successful attack by 20 of the squadron's Lancasters against the Arbergen rail bridge at Bremen, there was heavy flak. One of the BI (Special) Lancasters, PD117, YZ-L, was seen to be hit and set on fire. As YZ-L went down another Lancaster had to swerve out of the way of the falling aircraft. No parachutes were observed and the aircraft crashed south of Bremen killing the five-man crew of New Zealander, Flight Lieutenant Bernard Gumbly DFM.

On April 16, 1945, with only three weeks of the war to run, Squadron Leader John Powell DFC and his crew became the last 617 Squadron casualties of the war when their Lancaster, B III NG228, KC-V, was hit by flak during an attack against the German warships Prinz Eugen and the Lutzow at Swinemunde on the Baltic coast. One engine caught fire, the aircraft spiralled down out of control and the port wing broke off before it impacted the ground at Karsibor wood near Swinemunde. All seven of the crew were killed, the last of 183 men who gave their lives in the service of the squadron during the Second World War. The deaths of those like Powell and his crew, so close to the end of hostilities, seems particularly tragic.

The squadron's final operation of the war was a symbolic raid against the SS Barracks and Hitler's Eagle's Nest retreat at Berchtesgaden in the Bavarian mountains on April 25, 1945, as part of a force of more than 350 Lancasters from various other squadrons. The bombing was not as effective as usual, but all the squadron's Lancasters returned safely. On May 8, the war was over in Europe. No 617 was one of the squadrons detailed for the Tiger Force to go and fight the Japanese in the Far East, but before they could be deployed, two H-bombs of far greater power than Tallboy or Grand Slam were dropped by the Americans, the second of them observed by 617's old commanding officer, Group Captain Cheshire.

With the surrender of the Japanese, it really was over and 150 of the aircrew could suddenly, and in most cases unexpectedly, start to believe they had the same chance as ordinary people of living a long life.

With only three weeks of the war to run, John Powell and his crew became the last 617 casualties of the war.

Above: Three of 617 Squadron's Lancasters after the war in Europe. The squadron wore three sets of code letters. In the Dams Raid they wore AJ-, the unit's code then became KC-, but the B1 (Specials) wore YZ- codes. (© IWM MH30796)

Lancaster B1 DV385
Thumper Mk.III
of 617 Squadron

Above: RAF BBMF
Lancaster PA474 in the
colour scheme of 617
Squadron's DV385, KC-A,
Thumper Mk.III.
(© Richard Paver 2012)

One Lancaster that served with 617 Squadron from November 1943 until the end of the war was commemorated by the RAF Battle of Britain Memorial Flight Lancaster, PA474, for nearly five years. From September 2012 to June 2017, the aircraft was painted as Thumper Mk.III, with the code KC-A.

The story of the original aircraft and of the wartime pilot and crew who flew the majority of its operations encapsulates the squadron's history during the latter stages of the war.

Some of the modified Type 464 Lancasters which survived the Dams Raid remained in service with 617 Squadron but these aircraft were not suitable for all operations and the squadron needed replacement, standard Lancasters, as well as crews to make up losses. One of the new aircraft delivered to the unit was Lancaster BI DV385.

LANCASTER DV385

Lancaster DV385 was built by Metropolitan-Vickers Ltd at Trafford Park, Manchester, at a stage of the war when the average build time for a Lancaster was eight weeks. DV385 rolled off the production line in October 1943. It was delivered to 617 Squadron at RAF Coningsby (by a quirk of fate now home to the RAF BBMF Lancaster PA474) in November 1943 and given the squadron codes KC-A. The aircraft was retrofitted with bulged bomb-bay doors enabling it to carry one of the huge 12,000lb HC thin-case blockbuster blast bombs or, later, a 12,000lb Tallboy bomb, internally.

DV385's first bombing mission was flown on December 16, 1943; this was the first of four ops it flew from Coningsby, three of them captained by Flight Lieutenant Tom O'Shaughnessy, to drop 12,000lb HC bombs against V-weapon sites in France.

On January 9, 1944, 617 Squadron moved the few miles north to Woodhall Spa, taking DV385 with them.

BOB KNIGHTS AND HIS CREW

Another Lancaster squadron, 619, was already based at Woodhall Spa and moved to Coningsby to make way for 617 Squadron. One of the 619 Squadron crews, led by pilot Bob Knights, was coming towards the end of its tour at the close of 1943. Some of the crew were going to reach the 'magic' end-of-tour figure of 30 ops slightly before the others and they did not want to be split up, reasoning that they were safer together. So they had decided to volunteer for a second operational tour with 617 Squadron.

Knights and his crew were about to become very familiar with Lancaster DV385.

Robert 'Bob' Edgar Knights was born in January 1921 in London. He volunteered for service as a pilot with the RAF and was eventually called up in March 1941, aged 20. He completed his flying training in America under the Arnold Scheme, flying Stearman PT17s, Vultee BT13s and AT6A Texans. In May 1942, after returning to England to complete his training, he crashed in an Airspeed Oxford twin-engine aircraft. Bob badly injured his hand in the accident and this kept him off flying for six months.

In June 1943, with 474 hours' flying under his belt, Pilot Officer Bob Knights and his crew – Sergeants Rhude (navigator), Bell (bomb aimer), Twells (flight engineer), Rowan (wireless operator), Hobbs (mid-upper gunner) and Derham (rear gunner) – joined 619 Squadron to fly Lancasters on bombing operations.

Before he could fly operationally with his own crew, Bob Knights had to complete the traditional 'second dickey op' with an experienced crew to learn the ropes. He flew with Flight Lieutenant 'Ted' Dampier-Crossley DFC, a New Zealander in the Royal Australian Air Force, who was flying with the RAF on 619 Squadron. Dampier-Crossley's aircraft was Lancaster EE112, it wore the code letters PG-T (normally T for Tommy) and the crew had named it T for Thumper and painted the Walt Disney rabbit character, from the 1942 Walt Disney film Bambi on the nose.

Dampier-Crossley was an experienced operational bomber pilot and he taught Bob Knights some useful tricks and tactics, such as never flying straight and level but weaving constantly, which Bob's crew subsequently credited with helping to keep them alive.

Sadly, a couple of months later, on the night of August 10-11, 1943, Dampier-Crossley and his entire crew were killed during a raid on Nuremburg. A replacement Lancaster coded PG-T arrived on the squadron and was allocated to Knights and his crew, who decided to name it Thumper Mk.II in honour of Ted Dampier-Crossley.

The so-called Battle of Berlin began shortly afterwards and the Bob Knights crew made eight attacks against the 'Big City'; raids in which Bomber Command's losses were particularly high. One night the crew was en route to bomb Hamburg when one of the engines failed shortly after reaching the Dutch coast. They would have been justified in turning back, but pressed on and bombed the target successfully from only 10,000 feet.

He taught Knights some useful tricks and tactics, such as never flying straight and level.

Right: Bob Knights. (Author's Collection)

Below: Wg Cdr John Bell MBE DFC flew 27 of his 50 wartime 'ops' as a bomb aimer in the real Thumper Mk.III. His pilot, Bob Knights, taught him to fly the Lancaster and he is seen here in the pilot's seat of PA474. (RAF Coningsby Photographic Section. Crown Copyright 2012)

As a Lancaster had only a single pilot, Bob Knights decided that he would train his bomb-aimer, John Bell, to fly the aircraft in case he was killed or incapacitated. He felt that the bomb-aimer could most easily be spared from his other duties in such an eventuality. John Bell, who is the only surviving member of the crew, told the author, during a visit to the BBMF at Coningsby in September 2012, that he spent several hours in all at the controls of a Lancaster with Bob standing beside him advising him.

It is unlikely that such a novice Lancaster pilot, with no other piloting experience, would ever have been able to land the aircraft if his pilot was rendered 'hors de combat', but at least he might have been able to fly it back over friendly territory before the crew took to their chutes. John also said that he always seemed to over-control the aircraft, finding it difficult to keep it steady. When he was flying it, he said: "The rest of the crew were not best pleased!"

617 SQUADRON

Towards the end of 1943, as the crew was approaching the required 30 ops of a full operational tour with 619 Squadron, they volunteered for a second operational tour with 617 Squadron, even though they were due for a well-earned rest tour. After they had been interviewed by 617's commanding officer, Wing Commander Leonard Cheshire, the crew was posted to the elite unit in January 1944.

On the night of January 20, 1944, Flight Lieutenant Tom O'Shaughnessy, who had so far been the regular pilot of DV385 on 617 Squadron, was killed in a training accident at Snettisham, Norfolk, along with his navigator Flying Officer Holding. He was flying one of the original Type 464 Dams Raid Lancasters (ED918) and crashed into the sand dunes at the Wash bombing ranges, while practising for a proposed raid on an Italian dam that did not, in fact, go ahead.

After Tom O'Shaughnessy's death, DV385 needed a new crew and it was allocated to Bob Knights. He and his crew immediately decided that their new aircraft should be named Thumper Mk.III and the artwork – the cartoon rabbit holding a foaming pint of beer – was duly painted on the nose. They also started the 'bomb log' under the cockpit with a bomb symbol for each op successfully completed by Thumper Mk.III. The aircraft eventually flew 36 successful operations before it was retired from service in March 1945 (35 bomb symbols are painted on PA474 replicating a wartime photograph). It also flew an additional 13 sorties on which it reached the target, but circumstances prevented the bombs being dropped and they were brought back, as the Squadron's precision role sometimes demanded.

Bob Knights and his crew first flew Thumper Mk.III operationally on the night of February 8, 1944, as part of a force of 12 Lancasters which carried out an outstandingly accurate and successful night bombing raid against the Gnome-Rhone aero engine factory at Limoges. Four nights later the crew took part in a long-range attack on the Antheor viaduct, on the railway line between Toulon and Cannes, in an attempt to destroy the strategically important coastal rail link between France and Italy

Below: As she is today – Thumper Mk.III. (RAF Coningsby Photographic Section, Crown Copyright 2012)

The target was heavily defended and opposing ground fire was intense as the crew dropped their first 12,000lb HC bomb. During February, March and April 1944, mostly flown by Bob Knights, Thumper was used to attack factories and industrial sites producing vital war materials and equipment for the Germans. In April 1944, having completed more than 30 operations Bob Knights was awarded the DFC.

D-DAY – OPERATION TAXABLE

On the eve of D-Day, June 5-6, 1944, Knights and his crew flew Thumper Mk.III on the highly secret, deception raid, Operation Taxable (the op being recorded with a letter D on the bomb symbol on the aircraft's mission tally). The object of this operation was to convince the Germans that the main invasion fleet was heading for the Pas de Calais. Creating this illusion required the precise flying of elongated circuits, while bundles of radar-reflective, aluminium-foil strips of pre-determined and varying lengths – window – were dropped through the flare chute every five seconds. Another, similar, spoof operation, codenamed Glimmer, was conducted by Short Stirlings of 218 Squadron in the Boulogne area. Both were successful and, by daybreak on June 6, the German High Command was trying to react across an unnecessarily broad front. Many of the best German troops were kept on the wrong side of the Seine and the confusion caused by these operations undoubtedly helped the Allies to gain a vital foothold in Normandy on D-Day.

TALLBOY

On 15 occasions, 10 of them with Bob Knights at the controls, Thumper Mk.III was used to drop the 12,000lb Tallboy deep-penetration, earthquake bombs against high value targets.

Designed by Barnes Wallis, the Tallboy was a remarkable weapon, combining the explosive force of a large, high-capacity bomb and the penetrating power of armour-piercing munitions. When it was introduced it was the only weapon in the Royal Air Force's inventory capable of breaking through the thick concrete structures of the German U-boat shelters, E-boat pens and V-weapon sites.

Tallboy measured 21 feet (6 metres) long and contained 5200lb of Torpex explosive. With a streamlined (ogival) shape, it was fitted with a long, light-alloy, conical tail with four small square fins. These fins were offset by five degrees, causing the bomb to spin during its fall, aiding stability and improving its accuracy. To increase its penetrative power, the nose of the bomb contained a specially hardened and precisely machined, steel plug. Tallboy was ballistically perfect and in consequence had a very high terminal velocity. Released from an altitude of 18,000 feet, a Tallboy took only 37 seconds to fall to ground; when it hit, it was supersonic and still accelerating. It could penetrate 16 feet (5 metres) of concrete and made a crater 80 feet (24 metres) deep and 100 feet (30 metres) across, which would have taken 5000 tons of earth to fill. The bomb was designed to detonate below ground, transferring all of its energy into the target structure. This earthquake effect caused more damage than a direct hit, as it shook the whole target structure, causing major damage to all parts of it and making repair impossible or uneconomic. The fuses in the rear of the bomb could be set to give it sufficient time to penetrate before exploding. The time delay could be set to between 11 seconds and 30 minutes after impact.

Above: Armourers manoeuvring a Tallboy onto a bomb trolley. (© IWM CH 15363)

SAUMUR RAIL TUNNEL

The first time that the Bob Knights crew dropped a Tallboy from Thumper Mk.III was the operational debut for the new bomb on the night of June 8-9, 1944 (D-Day+2). The target for the new weapon was the Saumur railway tunnel in France, some 125 miles to the south of the Normandy battle area. This raid was prepared in great haste, as intelligence indicated that a German Panzer unit was expected to move by train through the tunnel. The aim was to prevent these and any other German reinforcements reaching Normandy from the south. The target area was illuminated with flares by four Lancasters of 83 Squadron and then marked at low level by two Mosquitos of 617 Squadron. 25 Lancasters of 617 Squadron, 19 carrying Tallboys, dropped their bombs with great accuracy. One Tallboy actually pierced the roof of the tunnel and brought down a huge quantity of rock and soil. The tunnel was blocked for a considerable period and the Panzer unit was badly delayed. No aircraft were lost on this raid.

STABILISING AUTOMATIC BOMB SIGHT (SABS)

To achieve accuracy with these large single bombs, 617 Squadron used a special bombsight – the Stabilising Automatic Bomb Sight (SABS) Mk.IIA – which, for the first time in the RAF's history, permitted true precision bombing from medium altitude. These special bomb sights were handmade, precision instruments, produced in small numbers and used only in specialist roles. With a well-trained and practiced bomb-aimer, able to keep the SABS aiming graticule exactly over the aiming point during the approach to the target, the sight automatically calculated the aircraft's ground speed and wind drift. These were the principal factors which led to inaccuracies with earlier bomb sights, like the Mk.XIV in use with the rest of Bomber Command.

The bomb was designed to detonate below ground. This earthquake effect caused more damage than a direct hit.

Above: Heading for Le Havre on June 14, 1944 for a daylight raid against E-Boat pens. Bob Knights in DV385 Thumper Mk.III KC-A flies in formation with Les Munro in his aircraft LM482 KC-W, each carrying a 12,000lb Tallboy bomb. (courtesy Les Munro)

The SABS fed information to a Bombing Direction Indicator mounted in front of the pilot, which showed him whether any course correction, left or right, was required. It also calculated the bomb release point and released the bomb automatically at the correct moment. Given optimum conditions, a well-trained crew could reliably place a bomb within 80 yards of the target from 18,000 feet. Achieving this level of precision required extremely accurate flying. Unfortunately, it also required a long straight run-up to the target of between five and 10 minutes, during which no evasive action was possible, making the Lancaster a sitting target for the defences, especially radar-directed 'predicted' flak. The combination of SABS and Tallboy was effective only if the aiming point could be clearly identified and tracked visually by the bomb aimer. Some missions were aborted or unsuccessful because this was not possible and, due to the cost and complexity of their manufacture, Tallboy bombs which were not dropped were brought back to base.

> *It required a long straight run-up to the target, making the Lancaster a sitting target for the defences.*

Thumper Mk.III bomb aimer, John Bell, said that the first time that they dropped practice bombs using the SABS, he scored direct hits on the aiming triangle on the bombing range in the Wash with the first two bombs. On the third run, John felt that things were not quite going right; he took over manually and missed the target by 75 yards. "I learned from that," he said, "the automatics were better than me." He went on to say: "When everything was going right there was no need for communication between the bomb aimer and the pilot, as the Bomb Direction Indicator mounted in front of the pilot gave him all the steering information needed. It was only if it drifted off that the bomb aimer needed to give the pilot heading corrections to make the pilot's indication live again."

THUMPER FIGHTS ON

During a daylight raid against E-boat pens at Le Havre on June 14, 1944 Thumper Mk III was hit by flak but only lightly damaged. It was flying again the next day, dropping a Tallboy against the E-boat pens at Boulogne.

Most of the aircraft's ops over the next few weeks were Tallboy raids against various V-weapon sites, including a V1 bomb store, various V2 rocket sites and the V3 long-range-gun construction site at Mimoyecques. John Bell remembers the direct hit with 'his' Tallboy on the north-west edge of the concrete dome at the V2 rocket site at Wizerne on July 17, 1944. He watched the bomb all the way down to impact. This attack caused severe damage to the site, which was still under construction. Three Tallboys, including the one dropped from Thumper, exploded next to the tunnels, one burst just under the dome, and another burst in the mouth of one tunnel. The whole hillside collapsed, undermining the dome support, and burying the entrances to the V2 launch tunnels. Although the concrete dome was unscathed, the buttresses supporting it were dislodged and the dome tilted, jeopardising the bunker from underneath. The site was abandoned a few weeks later (the site is now the La Coupole museum).

The last op that Bob Knights flew in Thumper was on August 5, 1944, dropping a Tallboy on the U-boat submarine pens at Brest. On August 7 he delivered the aircraft to Coningsby for servicing and modifications to be carried out; subsequently Lancaster LM482 KC-Q became his aircraft. This was the point at which bomb-aimer John Bell DFC left the crew and the squadron for a ground job. By this time he had flown 50 ops and decided enough was enough; his luck had held, but now was the time to stop. He became an admin (accounts) officer for six years and then he subsequently served as a photographic interpreter for the rest of his career, leaving the RAF on retirement in 1977 as a Wing Commander MBE DFC and with two Korean War medals.

TIRPITZ AND AFTER

Thumper Mk.III (now coded KC-V) returned to operations on October 3, 1944, piloted by Flying Officer James Castagnola (later Flight Lieutenant Castagnola DSO DFC). On October 28 and November 12 he captained Thumper on the final raids against the powerful German battleship Tirpitz, moored at Tromso. In common with all the Lancasters used on these missions, Thumper was modified for long-range flying. The mid-upper turret was removed along with many other internal fittings, and ex-Vickers Wellington overload fuel tanks were fitted, along with a Mosquito long-range tank, increasing the fuel capacity from 2154 to 2406 gallons, giving a range of 2250 miles. On the last of these missions, the Castagnola crew reported a direct hit with their Tallboy against the battleship's superstructure and the mighty ship capsized. For Thumper Mk.III the war was almost but not quite over, and a swastika on the 32nd bomb symbol on the mission log indicated a German fighter shot down by its gunners – its luck was still holding. The heavy-hitting bomber flew its last successful op dropping a Tallboy against the Bielefeld viaduct on February 22, 1945 and then, in March 1945, as the war approached its end, Thumper was retired. DV385 ended its life at 46 Maintenance Unit, where it was eventually struck off charge and scrapped after the war had ended.

BOB KNIGHTS DSO DFC

Bob Knights flew 41 ops with 617 Squadron, 29 of them in Thumper, and many of them among the unit's most challenging precision bombing operations. He also took part in all three Lancaster raids against the Tirpitz. In December 1944, after flying an official total of 67 bombing operations, Bob was rested.

In January 1945, he was awarded the DSO. During his 10 months with 617 Squadron, eight of the unit's Lancasters had failed to return from ops and another had been lost in an accident. Thirty-two of his fellow squadron aircrew had been killed and more had been injured or become prisoners of war. In April 1945 Bob was seconded to BOAC; he stayed with the airline for 32 years, retiring in 1976 as a Boeing 747 training captain.

Bob Knights DSO DFC died in December 2004, aged 83.

Left: Stunning at night, Thumper Mk.III. (RAF Coningsby Photographic Section, Crown Copyright 2012)

Below: Bob Knight's 617 Squadron crew after the successful attack on Tirpitz (Bob Knights is third from left). (Author's Collection)

Operations flown by Lancaster DV385 Thumper Mk.III

16.12.43	F/L O'Shaugnhessy	V1 Site at Pas de Calais 1x 12,000lb HC
20.12.43	S/L Martin	Liege Armament Works 1x 12,00lb HC
30.12.43	F/L O'Shaugnhessy	V1 Site at Pas de Calais 1x 12,000lb HC
04.01.44	F/L O'Shaugnhessy	V1 Site Pas de Calais 14x 1000lb
25.01.44	F/L Wilson	V1 Site at Pas de Calais 13x500lb + 3x 1000lb
08.02.44	F/O Knights	Limoges 11x 1000lb (Gnome-Rhone engine factory)
12.02.44	F/O Knights	Antheor viaduct 1x 12,000lb HC (severe ground fire)
02.03.44	F/O Knights	Albert 1x 12,000lb HC (aircraft factory – target wiped out)
04. 03.44	F/O Knights	St Etienne – No bombs dropped wx (needle bearing factory)
10.03.44	F/O Knights	St Etienne 11x 1,000lb (needle bearing factory)
15.03.44	F/O Knights	Woippy – Mission aborted wx (factory)
16.03.44	F/O Knights	Clermont Ferrand (Michelin tyre factory – v successful – div'd fog)
20.03.44	F/L Cooper	Angouleme 1x 8000lb + 1x 1000lb (explosive works)
23.03.44	F/L Fearn	Lyons 11x 1000lb (aero engine factory)
25.03.44	F/L Pryor	Lyons 12x 500lb (aero engine factory)
29.03.44	F/O Knights	Lyons 1x 8000lb + 2x 1000lb (aero engine factory)
5.04.44	F/O Knights	Toulouse AIA repair plant 1x 8000lb + 6x 500lb
		(this op not in 617 Sqn ORB – source Bob Knight's logbook)
10.04.44	F/O Knights	St Cyr 1x 8000lb + 6x 500 incendiaries (signals eqpt depot)
18.04.44	F/O Knights	Juvisy 6x 1000lb + 6 red spots (rail marshalling yards)
22.04.44	F/O Knights	Brunswick 1x 2000lb +10x clusters
24.04.44	F/O Knights	Munich (marking) Spot fires plus clusters
05.06 44	F/O Knights	Op Taxable (window) D-Day op
08.06.44	F/O Knights	Saumur Railway Tunnel 1x Tallboy
14.06.44	F/O Knights	E-Boat pens Le Havre 1x Tallboy. Hit by flak
15.06.44	F/O Knights	E-Boat Pens Boulogne 1x Tallboy
19.06.44	F/O Knights	Watten 1x Tallboy (V2 bunker)
20.06.44	F/O Knights	Wizernes – Op abandoned – recalled (again on 22.6.44)
24.06.44	F/O Knights	Wizernes 1x Tallboy (V2 rocket storage site)
25.06.44	F/O Knights	Siracourt 1x Tallboy (V1 bomb store)
04.07.44	P.O Saunders	Creil (V1 parts store in caves – tech prob bomb brought back)
06.07.44	F/L Pryor	Mimoyecques 1x Tallboy (V3 (gun) construction site)

17.07.44	F/O Knights	Wizerne 1x Tallboy (V2 rocket site) (DH NW edge of dome)
20.07.44	F/O Knights	Wizernes 1x Tallboy not dropped wx (V2 rocket site)
25.07.44	F/O Knights	Watten 1x Tallboy (V2 bunker)
31.07.44	F/O Knights	Rilly La Montagne (railway tunnel)1x Tallboy not dropped
		(target obscured by smoke/dust)
01.08.44	F/O Knights	Siracourt – Op abandoned wx
04.08.44	F/O Knights	Railway bridge at Etaples 12x 1000lb
05.08.44	F/O Knights	Submarine pens Brest 1x Tallboy (after this Knights flew LM492 Q')

DV385 delivered to Coningsby by Knights & F/O Twells only, on Aug 7, 1944.

DV385 was one of the ac modified for long-range flying for the forthcoming raids on Tirpitz. The conversion involved the removal of the mid-upper turret and many other internal fittings, and the fitment of ex-Vickers Wellington overload fuel tanks increasing fuel capacity to 2406 gallons and allowing 2250 miles range. DV385 was then coded V for Victor.

03.10.44	F/O J Castagnola	Westkapelle sea wall – no bombs dropped – target destroyed BBB
28.10.44	F/O J Castagnola	Tirpitz Tromso Fjord (1x Tallboy)
12.11.44	F/O J Castagnola	Tirpitz Tromso Fjord (1x Tallboy) direct hit centre of superstructure

Mid-upper turret re-fitted

| 08.12.44 | S/L JF Brookes | Urft dam – ac hit by flak over Dunkirk – did not bomb BBB |

DV385 now coded T for Tango

03.02.45	P/O J Castagnola	Poortershaven midget sub pens (1x Tallboy)
06.02.45	P/O J Castagnola	Bielefeld viaduct – abortive bomb not required BBB
08.02.45	F/O J Castagnola	Ijmuiden U-boat pens (1x Tallboy) – direct hit
14.02.45	S/L JF Brooks	Bielefeld viaduct – abortive bomb not required BBB
22.02.45	F/O J Castagnola	Bielefeld viaduct (1x Tallboy)
24.02.45	F/O J Castagnola	Dortmund-Ems canal abortive – did not bomb BBB
09.03.45	F/O J Castagnola	Bielefeld abortive – mission abandoned BBB
13.03.45	F/O J Castagnola	Bielefeld abortive – mission abandoned BBB
		(Note: BBB = bomb brought back)

TOTAL OPS: 50

TOTAL SUCCESSFUL OPS: 36 (35 ops on aircraft bomb log in wartime photo)

TALLBOYS DROPPED: 15

12,000lb HC DROPPED: 5

The RAF Battle of Britain Memorial Flight Lancaster B1 PA474 running its four Rolls-Royce Merlin engines at night to produce a spectacular image. This would have been a familiar scene at many RAF airfields in wartime. After the Dams Raid 617 Squadron re-equipped with standard Lancasters such as this, although the unit continued to operate some of the specially modified Type 464s that survived the raid. (Crown Copyright)

The other 617 Squadron VCs

During the Second World War the Victoria Cross (VC), Britain's highest award for gallantry, was awarded to 32 members of the RAF and Commonwealth Air Forces. Nineteen of those were to members of RAF Bomber Command; including 10 for Lancaster aircrew (five of these were awarded posthumously).

This number of VCs seems surprisingly low set against the thousands of aircrew involved in RAF bomber operations throughout the war. There were undoubtedly many examples of supreme courage in the face of the enemy which went unrewarded; some of them recorded in this publication.

Remarkably, among the 10 VCs awarded to Lancaster crew members, three of the recipients were pilots who served with 617 Squadron, which perhaps confirms the calibre of men that served with the unit. The first of 617's VCs was, of course, Wing Commander Guy Gibson VC, DSO and Bar, DFC and Bar, the squadron's first CO and leader of the Dams Raid; his story has already been told in full. One of the others, Flight Lieutenant William 'Bill' Reid, won his VC while flying a Lancaster with 61 Squadron, before he subsequently joined 617 in February 1944. The third of 617's VC recipients was the unit's third

CO, Wing Commander Leonard Cheshire. He is one of only five men, from the 51 who received the bronze cross for aerial operations, who won their award not for a single act of supreme valour but for an extended period of operational flying and prowess.

The stories of these other two 617 Squadron VCs are tales of remarkable men and outstanding courage, determination and skill. We tell them here:

FLIGHT LIEUTENANT WILLIAM 'BILL' REID VC

Bill Reid was a Scotsman, born in Baillieston, Glasgow in 1921, the son of a blacksmith. He received his main education at the Coatbridge Secondary School and then applied to join the RAF, starting his service in the RAF Volunteer Reserve (RAFVR) in August 1941. Reid completed his pilot training in Canada and the USA, receiving his wings and being commissioned as a pilot officer in June 1942.

On his return to the UK, Reid was screened as a flying instructor, no doubt in recognition of his flying skills. He found himself instructing on Vickers Wellington twin-engine bombers with a promise of an eventual posting to an operational Lancaster squadron. He got a taste of action one night in March 1943, while on a training cross-country navigation exercise, when his Wellington was attacked by a night fighter near Great Yarmouth. His aircraft was damaged on the port side as he took defensive action; he then diverted to Woolfox and when he landed he discovered that the port tyre had been hit, but he still managed to land safely.

Reid's promised operational posting did not materialise until July 1943, when he was sent to 1654 Heavy Conversion Unit at Wigsley near Newark for conversion to the Lancaster. He formed a crew – in the RAF's time-honoured method of self-selection – which consisted of: Flight Sergeant J W Norris (flight engineer), Flight Sergeant J A Jefferies (navigator), Flight Sergeant J J Mann (wireless operator), Flight Sergeant L Rolton (bomb aimer), Flight Sergeant D Baldwin DFM (mid-upper gunner) and Flight Sergeant A F 'Joe' Emerson (rear gunner). Reid flew his required 'second dickey' trip (to learn about operations) in a Lancaster of 9 Squadron on August 30, on a raid against Monchengladbach. He and his crew were then posted to 61 Squadron at Syerston and the crew flew their first op together on September 6, 1943. They had flown only nine operational sorties before the sortie that was to change Reid's life.

On the night of November 3, 1943, Reid and his crew took off from Syerston just before 5pm, flying Lancaster LM360 QR-O for Orange, as part of a force of about 600 bombers detailed to bomb Dusseldorf. He climbed steadily, heading towards Holland and crossed the Dutch coast at 21,000 feet.

Suddenly and without warning, O-Orange was attacked by a German ME Bf110 night fighter from dead astern. Reid's windscreen exploded in a blinding flash and he felt as if his head had been blown off. He was hit in the head and shoulder by slivers of shrapnel, and pieces of jagged Perspex from the shattered windscreen struck him in the body and face. Fortunately none of them penetrated his eyes although his eyelids were scratched and torn. Reid later said that the blow to his shoulder felt: "just like a hammer, not a spear". As he didn't think that he was going to lose consciousness he said: "I thought there was no point in talking much about it."

The cannon shells from the night fighter had badly damaged the Lancaster; the port elevator was severely damaged, several instruments were out of commission, the hydraulic systems were damaged and both gun turrets were affected. Half dazed by the impact to his head and face, Reid managed to get his goggles over his eyes to protect them from the howling, icy gale blowing through the shattered windscreen. Blood was flowing freely from his face and shoulder and he could taste it in his mouth, but the blast of cold air quickly coagulated the blood flow. Reid regained control of the aircraft at 19,000 feet. He told his crew that he felt all right when he was asked, as he could see no point in worrying them about his injuries. He checked that the rest of the crew were unharmed and calmly decided to continue his mission to Dusseldorf. In his mind this was not a particularly heroic decision, just a logical one, and he later said that he thought: "... it was safer to go on because we were still all flying in this big box of planes 10 miles wide and 10 miles deep, and it would have meant flying back through these and probably pranging into one. It was not a case of going on regardless. It was the safest thing to do."

To counteract the tendency of the aircraft to yaw to starboard because of the elevator damage, Reid had to apply a continuous, large amount of left rudder, which was very tiring. About a quarter of an

hour later, Lancaster O-Orange was attacked again. A FW 190 fighter bore in from the port beam and raked the whole length of the bomber's fuselage with a murderously accurate hail of cannon shells. The navigator, Jefferies, died instantly, crumpling to the floor while Mann, the wireless operator, fell on top of Jefferies, seriously wounded. Norris, the flight engineer, was wounded in his left forearm, and Reid was also hit again. Other shells ruptured the aircraft's oxygen and hydraulic systems, knocked out the intercom system, destroyed the compass and further damaged the two gun turrets.

Norris clipped an emergency oxygen bottle onto Reid's supply tube and then helped the pilot in holding the control yoke, as the badly damaged bomber slowly levelled out again at 17,000 feet. Reid calmly continued on his sortie, still determined to reach Dusseldorf. He had no compass now and no navigator to assist him, but he had memorised his route to the target. Navigating by the Pole Star until he recognised Cologne on the starboard side, he then turned for Dusseldorf. Flying with both arms folded around the control yoke, fingers linked, to hold the aircraft level, he began his final approach to the target, reaching the objective nearly an hour after the second night fighter

Above: Flt Lt Bill Reid VC. (© IWM CHP 795)

Opposite page: Bill Reid's medals. (Author's Collection)

As he didn't think he was going to lose consciousness he said: "I thought there was no point in talking about it."

> ## "The other thing on my mind was to get back because we had wounded. There was no way we could bale out with wounded."

Above: Bill Reid flew Lancasters with 61 and 617 Squadrons. (Lancaster PA 474 of RAF BBMF). (Crown Copyright)

attack. He had continued the flight in such a normal manner that the bomb aimer, Flight Sergeant Rolton, who was isolated in the nose compartment with no intercom, knew nothing of his captain's injuries or the other casualties in the crew. Their arrival over Dusseldorf was on time, Reid saw the marker flares go down and pointed the aircraft at them. As he held the Lancaster steady he felt the bombs release right over the centre of the target.

As Reid cleared the heavy flak zone, Rolton emerged from the bomb aimer's compartment to the chaos in the cockpit. He and Norris stood by Reid on the return flight, ready to help in controlling the aircraft if necessary. Navigating as best he could by the stars, Reid was steadily getting weaker now. The constant physical effort in keeping on hard left rudder, and holding the control column with both arms was sapping his remaining strength. He later said: "The other thing on my mind at the time was to get back because we had wounded on board. There was no way we could bale out with all the wounded. Because we had no oxygen in the system, the engineer gave me the little bottles that we carried, like small fire extinguishers, that you can clip on to your mask. Eventually we ran out. I wanted to get down below oxygen height, which is 10,000 feet, but I didn't want to come down too soon in case there was a big flak area that would shoot us down."

Near the Dutch coast they ran into a heavy flak barrage, but managed to get through without further damage or injury. Out over the North Sea, Reid descended to 7000 feet. Suddenly one of the four engines cut. Norris, light-headed from his own wounds and lack of oxygen, had forgotten to change

Below: Flt Lt Bill Reid's battle scarred Lancaster LM360 QR-O after he crash-landed at Shipdam on November 3, 1943 (note the open bomb bay doors). (Crown Copyright)

over the petrol cocks to a full tank, but instinctive training told him what was wrong and he swiftly rectified the fault. All engines resumed their former full power and the Lancaster levelled out to continue its flight home.

As he approached the English coast Reid, aware of the low petrol state of his aircraft and the ruptured hydraulics (the bomb doors had remained open after bombing and could not be retracted), decided to try to land at Wittering, where the extra length of available runway offered possible safety. Then he spotted a cone of searchlights, indicating an airfield below. Having no precise idea of his location, Reid circled the lights and flashed his landing lights to indicate his distressed aircraft condition; then prepared to land. With the hydraulic system damaged, Reid and Norris had to use the emergency compressed-air blow-down system to lower the undercarriage and flaps.

The descent into warmer levels had re-opened Reid's wounds. His head wound began bleeding freely again, threatening to obscure his vision. Rolton positioned himself behind his skipper, ready to pull him out and away from the control yoke if he lost consciousness or control. As the Lancaster touched down, the undercarriage collapsed and the bomber scraped along the concrete runway for about 60 yards before finally halting. They had landed at Shipdam in Norfolk, the base for the 44th Bombardment Group of the USAAF. It was one minute after 10pm.

Rescuers scrambled onto the Lancaster; they opened the ditching hatches on the top of the fuselage and got the crew out. As they were evacuated, Reid discovered for the first time that his navigator, Jefferies, was dead – shot through the head – and that Norris and Mann were wounded. All were taken away on stretchers and into an ambulance to be treated in the medical centre. Sadly, Mann, the wireless operator, died of his injuries the following day (he had been shot through the chest).

When Air Vice Marshal Cochrane, the AOC of 5 Group, heard the full story of the crew's epic flight to and from Dusseldorf, he promptly recommended the survivors for gallantry awards. Norris was awarded the Conspicuous Gallantry Medal and Emmerson (the rear gunner) the DFM. To his personal astonishment, Reid was notified that he was to receive the Victoria Cross (gazetted on December 14, 1943).

When he had recovered from his wounds, Reid was posted to 617 Squadron in February 1944, taking his bomb aimer, Les Rolton with him. On his first

flight back, Reid made a pig's ear of a landing and damaged the tail of the Lancaster. Wing Commander Cheshire, the commanding officer, apologised to him and said: "It's my fault. After all you have been through I should have given you a few circuits before you went off solo." Then he added that he would have to put a red endorsement into Reid's logbook. Many years later, Reid laughingly said: "I think I am the only pilot to get a Victoria Cross on one trip and a red endorsement on the next!"

Reid flew his first op with 617 Squadron on April 18, 1944. Subsequently, he took part in many of the squadron's successful raids, including Operation Taxable on the eve of D-Day; he dropped one of the first Tallboy bombs against the Saumur railway tunnel on June 8, and flew on various other Tallboy raids against V-weapon sites.

On July 31, 1944, Reid flew on a joint 617 and IX Squadron bombing raid on a V-weapon storage site in a railway tunnel at Rilly La Montagne, near Rheims. Over the target Reid released his Tallboy from 12,000 feet and was about to turn for home when his aircraft (ME557, KC-S) was hit in the fuselage and port wing by two 1000lb bombs, dropped from another Lancaster above them. One bomb ploughed through the aircraft in mid-fuselage, severing all control cables and fatally weakening the structure. Reid felt his control column go sloppy, realised what had happened and gave the order to bale out. As the rest of the crew came forward to abandon the Lancaster, the bomber fell into a flat spin, pinning Reid in his seat. Reaching overhead, he managed to release the cockpit escape hatch panel and struggled to get out.

Just as he emerged the Lancaster broke in two and Reid was flung out.

Landing safely by parachute, Reid was captured within the hour by German troops, and later met his wireless operator, Flying Officer Luker, also a prisoner. The other five members of the crew were killed: the two gunners had died in the rear part of the fuselage, while Les Rolton and the remaining two crew members perished in the forward section of the Lancaster. Reid was imprisoned in Stalag Luft III, Sagan, and was later moved to Stalag IV, Belleria, and finally to Luckenwald, near Berlin, where he was eventually released by the advancing Russians. He was repatriated to England in May 1945 on Operation Exodus – the Bomber Command air repatriation of prisoners of war from Europe.

Bill Reid left the RAF in 1946 and entered Glasgow University. He later attended the West of Scotland Agricultural College before travelling on a scholarship to India, North America, Australia and New Zealand. In 1950 he joined the MacRobert Trust Farms as an agricultural adviser. For more than 20 years he was the national cattle and sheep adviser for Spillers Farm Feeds. He retired in 1980 and moved to Crieff with his wife Violet who he married in 1952. When he married Violet, he had not told her of his VC. She was, he confessed, "a wee bit impressed" when she found out!

Bill Reid VC died in November 2001, aged 79.

Above: Local hero – Bill Reid VC visiting his home town of Baillieston in 1944.
(Reproduced by kind permission of Glasgow City Council, Libraries Information & Learning)

"I think I am the only pilot to get a Victoria Cross on one trip and a red endorsement on the next!"

GROUP CAPTAIN LORD CHESHIRE VC OM DSO AND TWO BARS DFC AND BAR

Of the five airmen who have been awarded the VC for gallantry over an extended period rather than for a single act of supreme valour, four were First World War combatants; the sole Second World War recipient in this category was Group Captain Leonard Cheshire.

Leonard Cheshire was born (appropriately) in Cheshire in 1917, the son of Dr Cheshire, Professor of Law and bursar at Exeter College, Oxford. He was educated at Dragon School, Oxford and Stowe, before starting a law degree at Oxford in October 1936. At university, Cheshire pursued the hedonistic pleasures of an undergraduate's life with relentless determination – fast cars, drinking bouts, decorative girlfriends and any escapade which provided an element of hidden danger. In 1937 he joined the Oxford University Air Squadron, probably in search of faster danger. His first flight, in an Avro Tutor from Abingdon, was on February 5, 1937, and he went solo on June 8. When his training was completed he was commissioned into the RAFVR in November 1937 and resumed his studies.

When the Second World War broke out Cheshire was mobilised and reported for further service and pilot training, receiving his wings on December 15, 1939. With promotion to flying officer on April 7, 1940, he completed final operational conversion and training at 10 OTU, Abingdon and Jurby, and on June 6 he arrived at Driffield, Yorkshire to join his first operational unit, 102 Squadron equipped with the ungainly Armstrong Whitworth Whitley bomber.

For the next five months, flying from 102 Squadron's various bases at Driffield, Aldergrove and Linton-on-Ouse, Cheshire gained invaluable

Above: Leonard Cheshire's medals. (Author's Collection)

Below: Cheshire was awarded his first DSO following a mission in an Armstrong Whitworth Whitley. (Author's Collection)

front-line experience of bombing operations. On the night of November 12-13, 1940, Cheshire flew Whitley P5005, N-Nuts, on a bombing mission against an oil refinery at Wesseling, near Cologne. When he found that the target area was blanketed by cloud, he decided to attack the railway marshalling yards at Cologne instead. As he ran in with the bomb doors open an anti-aircraft shell burst very close to the Whitley. There was a blinding explosion, the Perspex of the front turret was blown away and there was another terrific explosion in the fuselage. The shell had detonated a flare, which tore a 10 foot chunk out of the side fuselage. The aircraft caught fire, the control yoke was wrenched from Cheshire's hands and the cockpit filled with dense smoke. He regained control and the bomb load was released over the marshalling yards.

While Cheshire set course for home, thankful that the engines were still running, the rest of the crew fought the fire and eventually extinguished the flames. At one point the wireless operator, Henry Davidson, who had remained at his station throughout, appeared in the cockpit door with flames licking at his flying suit. The bomb-aimer beat out the flames with his hands. The smoke cleared and although the aircraft seemed to be flying rather erratically, Cheshire landed the Whitley safely back at base, with a gaping hole in its rear fuselage, after being in the air for eight and a half hours.

Despite being only a flying officer, Cheshire was awarded an immediate DSO and Sergeant Davidson was given the DFM.

In January 1941, Cheshire completed his first tour of operations, but immediately volunteered for a second tour. He was posted to 35 Squadron at Linton-on-Ouse. Newly re-formed in November 1940, 35 Squadron was the first unit to operate the Handley Page Halifax four-engine bomber. On March 7, Cheshire was awarded the DFC. The squadron flew its first operation with the new bomber on March 11-12, 1941, and the following month Cheshire received a bar to his DSO for, "outstanding leadership and skill on operations".

In the spring of 1941 he was detached for North Atlantic ferry work, a posting which effectively rested him in New York, where the bright lights and welter of hospitality reactivated his old hedonism. Cheshire tumbled into the glamorous company of the film star Constance Binney, 18 years his senior. Following a mad, whirlwind romance, they married; it was a disaster and did not last.

A return to operational flying in October 1941 was therapeutic for Cheshire and by the time that he completed his second tour of operations he had been promoted to squadron leader. He was posted as an instructor at 1652 Heavy Conversion Unit at Marston Moor in January 1942, before returning to operations for a third tour in September, as the officer commanding (OC) 76 Squadron, another

Halifax unit based at Linton-on-Ouse. By coincidence, 76 Squadron was the unit on which Cheshire's younger brother, Christopher, had been serving as a pilot when, on August 12-13, 1941, he had been shot down over Berlin and became a POW. Cheshire was now a wing commander with a second bar to his DSO. The squadron had recently suffered high losses and Cheshire immediately tackled the low morale on the unit. He realised that the performance of the Halifax could be improved by removing the mid-upper and front gun turrets, along with exhaust shrouds and other weighty non-essential equipment. These modifications allowed the Halifax to fly higher and faster; losses fell and morale rose accordingly.

On April 1, 1943 Cheshire left 76 Squadron and was appointed as the station commander of RAF Marston Moor with the rank of group captain. At the age of 25 he was, at the time, the youngest man in the RAF to hold such a responsible position. By September of that year Cheshire had discovered that the administrative duties of a station commander were not for him and he was desperate to return to operational flying. When the opportunity arose, he willingly reverted back to the rank of wing commander to become OC 617 Squadron in November 1943.

Cheshire was the right man at the right time to take command of 617 Squadron, with the unit still recovering from the disaster of the Dortmund-Ems canal debacle. He had the operational experience and credibility to lead the 'old lags' of 617 (a term Bomber Harris used to describe his experienced bomber aircrew), as the squadron evolved into the elite precision bombing and self-marking unit it was to become.

Cheshire landed the Whitley with a gaping hole in its fuselage, after being in the air for eight and a half hours.

As a character Cheshire could not have been more different from the squadron's first CO – Gibson. Cheshire did not look the part at all. Indeed, he looked more like a theological student dressed as a senior officer. In contrast to Gibson's stocky frame, he was tall, lean and angular. Whereas Gibson was impatient and often aloof, Cheshire was even-tempered and unreserved. He was a strange blend of brilliant, if somewhat erratic intellect, self-consciousness, confidence and soft-spoken charm. He was highly sensitive and could be introspective; he had a gentle consideration for other people and yet in an aircraft cockpit he was cool, efficient and calculating. He seemed to radiate a fearlessness that somehow never came across as arrogance. His ability to instil confidence in his crew members meant that the question of whether they would get back never seemed to arise. Cheshire did not have a shred of social superiority; he was comfortable with all ranks and they all liked him, and yet his warm-hearted attitude never seemed to undermine his natural authority. For two days after he arrived as OC 617 Squadron, Cheshire did not realise that the WAAF sitting in a shooting brake outside his office was, in fact, his driver, until she told him. He had been walking everywhere as he hadn't expected to have a car and a driver at his disposal. It was fairly typical of the man that he never took for granted what some lesser men demanded. Like the unit's first CO, Cheshire had a dog that did tricks, but his was a large white poodle, called Simon!

The development of the squadron's precision bombing and low-level target marking techniques with the introduction of new specialist equipment including the SABS bomb sight and the Tallboy deep penetration bombs, has been fully covered elsewhere in this publication. So has the way in which Cheshire rapidly converted to the DH Mosquito and to the P-51 Mustang to further improve the unit's operational capabilities. He led virtually every squadron raid himself and brought the art of target marking and the concept of Master Bomber to a high peak of efficiency and effectiveness. He sometimes operated the Mosquito to the absolute limit of its fuel endurance and through withering anti-aircraft fire.

The citation for Cheshire's VC, which was announced on September 8, 1944, highlighted an operation Cheshire flew to Munich on April 24, 1944, in Mosquito FB6 MS993, without under-wing fuel drop tanks, as they could not be acquired in time:

"This was an experimental attack to test out the new method of target marking at low level against a heavily defended target situated deep in enemy

Above: Cheshire (centre front) with his 35 Sqn Halifax crew and ground crew at Linton-on-Ouse in early 1941. (© IWM CH 6373)

Below: Halifax Mk.I L9530 MP-L near its Middleton St George base flown by Flt Lt Christopher Cheshire. His luck ran out in August 1941, when it failed to return from Berlin. (© IWM COL 185)

He became a carer for ex-serviceman, and dedicated his life to supporting sick and disabled people.

territory. He was obliged to follow, in bad weather, a direct route which took him over the defences of Augsburg and thereafter he was continuously under fire. As he reached the target, flares were being released by our high-flying aircraft and he was illuminated from above and below. All guns within range opened fire on him. Diving to 700 feet he dropped his markers with great precision and began to climb away. So blinding were the searchlights that he almost lost control. He then flew over the city at 1000 feet to assess the accuracy of his work and direct other aircraft. His own was badly hit by shell fragments but he continued to fly over the target area until he was satisfied that he had done all in his power to ensure success. Eventually when he set course for base the task of disengaging himself from the defences proved even more hazardous than his approach. For a full 12 minutes after leaving the target area he was under withering fire, but he came safely through."

What the wartime citation does not say about this operation was that Munich was very much at the limit of the range of a Mosquito without drop tanks. When Cheshire finally landed from the mission he had been airborne for four hours and 37 minutes on the aircraft's internal fuel alone and had only 10 minutes of fuel remaining. The VC citation went on to say: "Wing Commander Cheshire has now completed a total of 100 missions. In four years of fighting against the bitterest opposition he has maintained a record of outstanding personal achievement, placing himself invariably in the forefront of the battle. What he did in the Munich operation was typical of the careful planning, brilliant execution and contempt for danger which has established for Wing Commander Cheshire a reputation second to none in Bomber Command."

Although Cheshire's VC was announced on September 8, 1944, he did not receive it from the King at Buckingham Palace until November 13, 1945. Two days after his VC was promulgated and now promoted to group captain again, he left England bound for India and the Eastern Air Command HQ at Calcutta. On August 9, 1945, Cheshire was in the third B-29 to fly to Nagasaki to witness the effects of the second atom-bomb attack. At the end of 1945 Cheshire's health began to break down. Like Britain herself, he had been fighting or training for fighting since 1939 and he was told that he was now suffering from psycho-neurosis. At his request he was discharged from the RAF in January 1946.

Leonard Cheshire is at least as well known for his charitable works after the war as he is for his wartime exploits. His early searches for 'direction' saw him becoming a carer for a terminally ill ex-serviceman, and led to him dedicating the rest of his life to supporting sick and disabled people. He turned to Christianity and was received into the

Roman Catholic Church in 1948. In 1959 he married fellow Catholic convert and humanitarian Sue Ryder (later Baroness Ryder of Warsaw), founder of the renowned charity shops and homes. In the meantime his Leonard Cheshire Foundation Homes for the Sick (Cheshire Homes) – providing accommodation, services and support for disabled people – were steadily multiplying. Eventually there were 270 Cheshire Homes in 51 countries. (The charity is now known as Leonard Cheshire Disability.)

Cheshire was awarded the Order of Merit (OM) in 1981 and a life peerage as Baron Cheshire of Woodhall in 1991 (he and Baroness Ryder were one of few married couples to both hold titles in their own right). Group Captain Lord Cheshire VC OM DSO and two Bars DFC and Bar, died of motor neurone disease on July 31, 1992, aged 74.

Above: Gp Capt Leonard Cheshire VC. (© IWM CH 13626)

Our artist tells history
Phil Tetlow's work, in his words

Below: The proportions and framing of the image on the finished page were prime considerations for Phil.

Phil Tetlow, who painted the stunning cover picture specifically for this publication, is a Lincolnshire-based artist with a wide repertoire that includes landscape paintings, portraits, aviation art and other commissions.

Phil graduated in fine art at Sheffield College of Art and Brighton before teaching art in Yorkshire and Lincolnshire. He now exhibits widely throughout the UK. He says that he is of the generation of painters who were trained in a traditional way and he acknowledges the influence of Paul Henry, Alfred Munnings and the impressionists on his style.

One of Phil's common themes in his diverse work is light and its ever changing effects on the landscape, buildings and

With that iconic raid in May 1943 there is a wealth of documentation both contemporary and modern.

people. Phil loves huge open skies and sudden seasonal changes, saying: "I want to capture that instant play of light on the landscape, the contrasting tones, the dapples and reflections. Although essentially anchored in realism, each piece represents my striving to balance an image of reality with the pure enjoyment of the physical process involved, maintaining the painterly qualities and enabling my work to be appreciated on many levels."

Many of Phil's aviation paintings are action scenes and when I invited him to paint a picture for use on the cover of this publication he readily agreed. I asked him to keep notes during the process of painting the picture to give an insight into his thought processes and his techniques. The final result is a dramatic picture, which fits the purpose superbly, and a fascinating description of the background to it.

OVER TO PHIL:

The Dambusters: Where do you start? It is probably the most popular subject for aviation artists. The scene has been portrayed from every angle.

The first thing I do when starting any aviation subject is to research the event thoroughly. With many of my previous subjects this has been difficult, but with that iconic raid in May 1943 there is a wealth of documentation both contemporary and modern.

Stage 1

Stage 2

Viewers and purchasers of aviation art often have great knowledge themselves and any anomalies or anachronisms are swiftly leapt upon. Details of the aircraft used are plentiful and easily accessed. Nowadays, due to modern technology, images of the dams are also easily resourced. As the landscape around them has changed little in the past 70 years and the raid took place on a moonlit night, representing them as they were should present few problems. Indeed, the possibility of showing them from different angles can be based on the photographs available.

Although it is possible to use a landscape format and then crop a suitable section for a vertical format book, I decided to work directly into a vertical format using a 3x2 ratio. This is partly because I wanted to retain more control over the finished result and also because many of my landscape paintings have used a vertical format.

There followed a series of sketches to try to arrange the various elements in a dynamic and original composition. A view from the ground or the air? Dam or aircraft as the dominant feature? Which dam? Which aircraft? Viewed from the front, rear or side? Lighting, moon in the south or south east, searchlights? Flak effects?

Once these decisions are made the accuracy of the aircraft has to be considered. Angles and proportions have to be spot-on, as with any well-known and iconic aircraft any slight inaccuracy stands out immediately to a critical observer. My usual way of avoiding this is to use accurate models. I use at least 1:48 scale to get the detail I need selecting the angle of view and also the distance the subject is viewed from. Any artist

Left: The moon area is given lighter tones in Stage 1, while darker tones are then added (above) in Stages 2 and 3 (below right).

Above right: Phil hard at work in his studio.

Angles and proportions have to be spot-on, as any slight inaccuracy stands out immediately to a critical observer.

Stage 3

Stage 4

knows that the viewing distance will greatly influence the perspective effect. Fortunately, I already have a 1:48 scale Tamiya Lancaster BIII from a previous project, not the Dambuster Type 464 Upkeep version, but this amendment should not be difficult to achieve with the amount of images available. A combination of drawings and photographs will then be used to achieve the desired effect.

Reference to Google Earth established the orientation of the dam which gave a rough position of the moon during the raid. As the chief source of light to the scene this was vital... but its position was also integral to the composition from an artistic point of view. The model Lancaster was positioned as required and illuminated from behind to simulate the desired effect of the moonlight on the aircraft. For the landscape a series of contemporary photographs gave the accuracy required but the effect of the moonlight relied on my own artistic interpretation.

The canvas used is 20 x 30 inches, used in the vertical format and before the composition was sketched out the entire sky area was blocked in with a mixture of phthalo blue and cerulean. After drying, this was graduated to lighter tones around the moon area (Stage 1). It is important to eliminate all the blank canvas early so the ground and water areas were blocked in with dark tones once they had been sketched in (Stages 2 and 3). Final balancing of the composition would be achieved when all the elements were in place.

Positioning the aircraft was critical as the whole composition depended on it. It had to appear that it was banking round after the final attack, giving a dynamic effect while balancing the composition. Once positioned the aircraft was blocked in with Payne's grey giving a silhouette on to which highlights would gradually be added, roundels and squadron codes would also be added (Stages 4 and 5 – left and below).

Stage 5

All the elements were now in place and time was spent balancing the foreground and background images tonally and gradually adding appropriate detail. One of the most daunting tasks is the water effect as the dam finally collapsed. Contemporary images show a large surge of water several hours after the raid, so the effect immediately after the final attack must have been quite spectacular.

The aspect of the feature Lancaster meant that the two spotlights used to ascertain the height of the aircraft during the attack had to be accurately positioned on the airframe. Research uncovered a diagram indicating their relative positions and angles. This was confirmed by a second diagram which had excellent provenance, the A V Roe Company itself. Likewise, the specially designed bomb cradle was represented using contemporary photographs and structural diagrams.

The aircraft represented is Lancaster ED906, AJ-J, flown by Flight Lieutenant David Maltby DFC, which struck the final blow to breach the Möhne dam. By this time most, if not all the light flak had ceased firing, but both Gibson and Martin circled the area to draw off remaining fire. I included them in the distance to balance the composition and add drama and depth (Stage 6, below).

My usual technique in the final stages of any painting is to remove the painting from the studio and place it where I am seeing it regularly and, to a certain extent, with fresh eyes. I make notes of any improvements and adjustments required and every few days return to the studio to carry them out. Although this can sometimes go on for quite a while, eventually I will reach the point where no further amendments are required and the work can be varnished. This has the effect of strengthening the colours and increasing the contrast.

■ www.philtetlow-artist.com

Stage 6

Opposite page, bottom left, and left: More of Phil's stunning work.

Last one home

In the breaking light of dawn, Lancaster ED886 AJ-O, flown by Flight Sergeant Bill Townsend and his crew, limps home across the North Sea on three engines.

Having dropped their Upkeep against the Ennepe dam (modern research suggests that it may actually have been the Bever) the crew had experienced an epic low level flight home as the sun came up. They penetrated a barrage of anti-aircraft fire as they coasted out over Holland and then, when they were over the North Sea, an oil pressure problem forced them to shut down one of the Lancaster's engines. They eventually landed back at Scampton at 06:15, the last of the 11 aircraft to return from the 19 that set out on the mission.

In the footsteps
of the Dambusters

Above: Model Lancaster in the RAF Scampton Heritage Centre.
Below: No.1 hangar, the home of Scampton's heritage centre.
(Both courtesy Flt Lt Sarah James)

During the Second World War 617 Squadron was based in the county of Lincolnshire – 'Bomber County' – and today there are many aviation heritage sites in the county which have Dambusters links. Visitors to Lincolnshire can 'fill their boots', to use an RAF expression, with Dambusters history.

SCAMPTON

617 Squadron was formed at RAF Scampton on March 21, 1943, specifically for a one-off special mission. After several weeks of intensive training flying from the base, the Dams Raid was launched from Scampton's grass airfield on the night of May 16, 1943. As we know, eight of the 19 aircraft sent on the raid did not return. After the raid, 617 Squadron remained at Scampton until August 1943, when the station was closed for the construction of hard runways, and the unit moved to RAF Coningsby.

Today it is possible to visit RAF Scampton, with the kind permission of the station commander, despite it still being a current operational RAF base and home to the RAF Aerobatic Team, the world famous Red Arrows. The RAF Scampton Heritage Centre was inaugurated in 1993 to commemorate the history of the famous station and as a tribute to those who have served there over its long history. Originally, the museum was housed in the building that had once been the station's main briefing room and where the Dams Raid crews were briefed for the mission.

After several moves, the museum is now located in the airfield-side annex accommodation of No. 1 Hangar, one of the original Second World War hangars.

The museum is run on a voluntary basis and access is by pre-arranged guided tour only. Entry to the museum is free to the general public, but, as the museum is not permanently manned and due to current security measures, access to the station is not possible without prior arrangement.

The centre's volunteers provide guided tours of the station, throughout the year, to view the exterior of the historic buildings on the technical site, including the front façade of the officers' mess and the outside of the wartime briefing room, and also to see the grave of Guy Gibson's famous dog which was run over and killed in front of the station's main gates on the night before the Dams Raid. Tours finish at the museum in No. 1 Hangar, which houses more than 700 items pertaining to the station's history, including an original half-size trial Upkeep bomb. However, the museum is not just about 617 Squadron and the Dams Raid; it also covers the history of the base from 1917 up to the present day. Featured prominently is the station's role as a V-Force base for the Vulcan, equipped with its Blue Steel missile, an example of which is on show.

For more information and details on how to book a tour, visit the website at www.raf.mod.uk/rafscampton

Tours finish at the museum in No. 1 Hangar, which houses more than 700 items pertaining to the station's history.

Pictured: Exhibits at the RAF Scampton Heritage Centre. (Pictures courtesy Flt Lt Sarah James)

Below: The grave of Guy Gibson's famous black labrador dog, run over and killed at the station's main gates on the night before the Dams Raid. (A Carty – GNU free documentation license)

WOODHALL SPA

RAF Woodhall Spa was home to 617 Squadron from January 1944 until the end of the Second World War in Europe. It was from here that the squadron operated throughout the 'Cheshire era' and subsequently under Tait and Fauquier, departing and returning from the airfield for most of its major raids of the war.

Constructed on land about one kilometre south of Woodhall Spa village, the airfield was built in 1941 with paved runways, as a satellite airfield to RAF Coningsby. Some of the original woodland was retained in the north-eastern part of the airfield and some parts of the new airfield, including the bomb store, were built into the woodland for cover. The main technical site was located on the southern side of the airfield, near Tattershall Thorpe village, with a type T2 hangar. The dispersed camp accommodation was built just south of the airfield, mostly in Tattershall Thorpe, and consisted of two communal sites, six domestic sites and the sick quarters. RAF Woodhall Spa opened for business in February 1942.

Today the runways are gone, replaced by a sand and gravel quarry which is now Woodhall Spa Airfield Nature Reserve, although the RAF continues to hold part of the old airfield as a satellite site to Coningsby, albeit for component servicing and storage. The wooded area to the north of the airfield is now the Forestry Commission's Ostler's Plantation and is open to walkers. Nature is slowly reclaiming the wartime concrete hard-standings and tracks, and the brick buildings, but intriguing glimpses of the past can still be found in the woods, particularly part of the bomb dump and an aircraft hard-standing with tie-down rings.

Part of the former RAF Woodhall Spa domestic site has been given new life as the Thorpe Camp Visitor Centre. The centre was formerly part of No. 1 Communal Site, RAF Woodhall Spa, and when it was built in 1941 it had a planned lifespan of only 10 years. The site included the officers' and sergeants' messes, airmen's dining halls and the NAAFI building, together with ration stores, latrine and ablution blocks. Only the airmen's dining halls, the NAAFI and ration store are within the centre's current boundary.

Above: Thorpe Camp. This photo taken on a snowy January day gives an impression of the harsh living conditions experienced by those who lived at RAF Woodhall Spa's No 1 Communal Site during the winter.

Below: The Petwood Hotel was the Officers' Mess for 617 Sqn officers at Woodhall Spa. (both Author's Collection)

At the end of the war, when the RAF vacated the site, it became a target for squatters and was then taken over by the local council and converted into temporary housing. Several of the buildings have been returned to their original condition and now house displays depicting the stories and history of RAF Woodhall Spa. The entrance to the Thorpe Camp Visitor Centre is guarded by a small memorial dedicated to 97, 617, 619 and 627 Squadrons. It is topped by a bent propeller from an Avro Lancaster, which was recovered from The Wash. This was originally erected on the airfield in 1993 by the officers and airmen of the Propulsion Flight, RAF Woodhall Spa; it was moved to Thorpe Camp Visitor Centre when the Propulsion Flight closed in 2003. Other displays are devoted to Civilian Life in Lincolnshire during the Second World War, Lincolnshire's involvement in Arnhem, and The Air Training Corps. The centre also has a complete BAC Lightning Mk.I on show.

Thorpe Camp Visitor Centre is open every Sunday and Bank Holiday Monday from Easter to the end of October and on Wednesdays during July and August from 1-5pm. Guided tours can be arranged for organised groups at other times. For more information see thorpecamp.wixsite.com/visitorscentre

While the officers of the other squadron at RAF Woodhall Spa – 627 Squadron – and the NCOs and airmen of both squadrons 'slummed it' in the temporary hutted accommodation at Tattershall Thorpe, the officers of 617 'lorded it' in their requisitioned mess at the Petwood Hotel in Woodhall Spa – a fine mock-Tudor building which had originally been the home of Sir Archibald and Lady Weigall.

Today the Petwood retains a compelling sense of history. Taking tea or having a drink on the terrace, overlooking the large grounds, it is easy to imagine the aircrew of 617 Squadron doing exactly the same during some off-duty moments in wartime. The hotel's Squadron Bar, rarely used as a bar, is dedicated as a tribute to those men and has an interesting range of memorabilia. Indeed, the public areas are full of paintings and pictures of 617 Squadron subjects. The Petwood is still the natural home for 617 Squadron and squadron reunions are held there every year.

The 617 Squadron Association meets twice a year in Woodhall Spa; in May to commemorate the Dams

Right: The 617 Sqn memorial in the centre of Woodhall Spa bears the names of all those who gave their lives in the service of the squadron during the Second World War and the squadron's wartime battle honours. (Author's Collection)

The Petwood retains a compelling sense of history. Taking tea, it is easy to imagine the aircrew doing the same.

Raid, and on the Remembrance Weekend in November to commemorate the sinking of the German battle cruiser Tirpitz and to join with the local community in honour comrades who have passed away.

Woodhall Spa town did not escape the effects of the war being fought from their doorstep by the airmen for whom the town had become a temporary home. The town was on the receiving end of the German war machine and suffered several air attacks, the most notable being on August 17, 1943, when two parachute mines fell near the centre of the village. The Royal Hotel was all but flattened and several people were killed. The bombed-out site was not subsequently built upon and is now the location of the magnificent 617 Squadron war memorial, which takes the form of a breached dam.

The dam walls bear the names of those members of the squadron who gave their lives during the Second World War; the squadron's battle honours are inscribed on the 'waters' flooding through the breached dam.

Since the end of the Second World War, over 30 additional members of 617 Squadron have died serving their country either with the squadron or with other units. In addition, the squadron has won two additional battle honours. In 2010, to commemorate these servicemen, the 617 Squadron Aircrew Association drew up plans to erect a second memorial at the same site, adjacent to its Second World War memorial. Erected and unveiled in May 2013, to commemorate the 70s anniversary of the Dams Raid, this takes the form of a 3m high black granite pyramid, its shape echoing the wing form of two of the aircraft flown postwar by the squadron – the Vulcan and Tornado. A projecting triangular pediment carries the squadron badge and the inscription 'In memory of all members of 617 Squadron RAF who gave their lives since 1945 in the service of their country. We will remember them'.

The polished side faces of the pyramid contain inset red glass lightning flashes, the symbol carried on the squadron's Tornado GR4 aircraft during the 1990s and 2000s, and would be inscribed with the squadron's battle honours of 'Gulf 1991' and 'Iraq 2003'.

EAST KIRKBY – LINCOLNSHIRE AVIATION HERITAGE CENTRE

While not actually part of 617 Squadron history, with the exception that Wing Commander Guy Gibson served there as a staff officer at HQ 55 Base for a few weeks in mid-1944, no trip to Bomber County is complete without a visit to the Lincolnshire Aviation Heritage Centre (LAHC) at East Kirkby – a privately owned, family run museum.

It is now widely seen as a living memorial to all the 55,500 men of Bomber Command who lost their lives during the Second World War, including the brother of the founders, farmers Fred and Harold Panton.

Christopher Panton was a flight engineer who was killed when his Halifax bomber was shot down on a raid to Nuremberg at the end of March 1944.

The LAHC is the only airfield museum in Britain recreated to its original design, sited on an original Second World War airfield, allowing the visitor to get the feel for the atmosphere. One of the main features of the site is the original air traffic control tower, where you can listen to the recreated R/T as the bombers return from Berlin. A display in the tower pays respect to the WAAFs who were a very important but often forgotten part of the operation. The centre's collection also includes many wartime vehicles, including a Ford WOT1 Crew Bus, the only one of its kind known to exist.

The large hangar is relatively new, although built on the original base, and houses the centre's jewel in the crown, Avro Lancaster Bomber, NX611 Just Jane, which frequently performs four-engine taxi runs. Just Jane is one of only two Lancasters in the UK able to move under its own power and although currently restricted to taxi runs, the museum has plans

Above: The original, restored control tower at the LAHC, East Kirkby. (Courtesy LAHC)

Below: The Upkeep bouncing bomb at the East Kirkby museum. (Author's Collection)

Below and below left: Lancaster NX611 *Just Jane* conducts regular taxy runs. LAHC has announced its intention to return the bomber to airworthy status. (Courtesy LAHC)

Below: The graves of Fg Off John Dempster and Fg Off John Gordon in Coningsby cemetery. They died in a flying accident in February 1944.
(Author's Collection)

Below right: The six RAF BBMF Spitfires, one of the Hurricanes and Lancaster PA474, on display outside the Flight's hangar at RAF Coningsby.
(Crown Copyright)

to return the bomber to airworthy status over the next few years. Also housed in the hangar is one of the largest private collections of wartime photographs. In addition, cabinets contain original equipment used by each crew member on the aircraft and by the ground crew. Also displayed in the hangar are the many parts of aircraft recovered by the Lincolnshire Aircraft Recovery Group and an original trial Upkeep bouncing bomb.

Although the museum is built up entirely around RAF Bomber Command, the exhibits and displays span many areas such as The Home Front and Escape and Evasion, giving a wide perspective on the trials and tribulation of the Second World War.

The Lincolnshire Aviation Heritage Centre is open all year Monday to Saturdays (closed Sundays). For more information visit www.lincsaviation.co.uk

CONINGSBY AND THE BATTLE OF BRITAIN MEMORIAL FLIGHT

RAF Coningsby was the home base for 617 Squadron after it moved from Scampton in August 1943 and until the unit settled at Woodhall Spa in January 1944. It was from Coningsby that the squadron launched the disastrous Dortmund-Ems canal raid of September 15-16, 1943, from which only three of the eight aircraft returned. The squadron was still at Coningsby when Leonard Cheshire arrived as the new commanding officer in November 1943.

Following the brown tourist signs from Coningsby village, past its ancient church with its one-handed clock on the tower, the visitor drives past a cemetery on the way to the Battle of Britain Memorial Flight Visitor Centre. Most will pass by without a glance,

but, as with most cemeteries adjacent to RAF airfields, among the graves are some belonging to RAF personnel. Hidden in the far corner are 60 or so clean, white headstones arranged in four rows, dating from between 1939 and 1988. Among them are the graves of two airmen who died flying with 617 Squadron in 1944.

On the night of February 12, 1944, 10 Lancasters of 617 Squadron took off from Woodhall Spa to land at Ford (on the south coast of England, in West Sussex) so that they could refuel and launch from there for a long-range mission to bomb the Antheor viaduct in southern France. After the raid, the returning aircraft landed at Ford to refuel again. One of the Lancasters, DY382 AJ-J, was slightly delayed in taking off for Woodhall Spa and by the time it did, the weather had deteriorated. The captain, Squadron Leader Suggitt DFC, decided that despite the fog, he could make it back to Woodhall. Shortly after take-off the aircraft crashed into a hill 10 miles northeast of Chichester. Six of the crew members were killed in the crash, along with a passenger, the Woodhall Spa Station Intelligence Officer Squadron Leader Lloyd DSO. One of the dead was Flight Sergeant John Pulford, who had been Guy Gibson's flight engineer on the Dams Raid. Squadron Leader Suggitt was pulled from the wreckage alive, but died a few days later. The graves of Flying Officer John Gordon DFC, the 31-year-old navigator, and Flying Officer John Dempster DFC, the 20-year-old rear gunner, are in the Coningsby cemetery.

Today RAF Coningsby is still a thriving, busy and fully operational base, now with Typhoon fighters flying from the airfield. Between them, Coningsby's resident units operate the RAF's newest and oldest

aircraft because the station is also the home of the RAF Battle of Britain Memorial Flight (RAF BBMF) with its fleet of historic, Second World War aircraft.

The RAF BBMF is a regular unit, manned by RAF personnel and funded by the Ministry of Defence. Sometimes referred to as a 'museum without walls', it maintains a fleet of 12 historic and irreplaceable aircraft in airworthy condition, including Avro Lancaster PA474, currently one of only two airworthy Lancasters in the world. Before it's most recent repainting as W5005 'AR-L' 'Leader', PA474 was painted to represent a Lancaster of 617 Squadron – DV385 KC-A, Thumper Mk.III. The BBMF fleet also includes a C-47 Dakota, six Spitfires, two Hurricanes and two de Havilland Chipmunk training aircraft. Some of these aircraft have remarkable wartime pedigrees and all have defied the odds to survive in flying condition.

The RAF BBMF exists to commemorate the personnel of the Royal Air Force who have served their country in conflict, particularly during the Second World War, and especially those who gave their lives for the freedom of others. The flight's fleet of Second World War aircraft is preserved in flying condition as a living tribute to them all.

In a partnership between the RAF and county council, the BBMF Visitor Centre has provided the public with a gateway to the home of the RAF BBMF for more than 32 years, allowing them the opportunity to view the aircraft at close quarters. Because it is a working environment and not a museum, entry to the hangar is by guided tour only. The knowledgeable and enthusiastic guides, who lead groups around the hangar, are all volunteers. Many have served with the Armed Forces and some have first-hand crew experience of the aircraft they are talking about. All of them are keen to ensure that the public appreciate this living tribute to the RAF aircrews and ground crews who played their part so courageously during the Second World War.

The BBMF display season normally runs from the beginning of May to the end of September, with pre season work-up training for the crews taking place in April, culminating in public display approval being granted to each pilot by the air officer commanding. During the display season all the aircraft fly regularly and some aircraft may be away on display duties. Between flights and away trips, routine servicing and rectification work takes place in the hangar. During each display season the memorial flight is typically tasked to fly over 100 displays and it conducts around 300-400 flypasts at other events of all shapes and sizes, generating 1000 individual aircraft appearances per year.

The BBMF Visitor Centre has a rare Grand Slam and a Tallboy bomb on display out in the open, allowing the sheer scale of these awesome weapons to be appreciated. The BBMF Visitor Centre is open year round on weekdays only, with occasional weekend opening. For opening times, parking and access information, and other details, visit www.lincolnshire.gov.uk/visiting/museums/battle-of-britain-memorial-flight or alternatively www.raf.mod.uk/bbmf/visitorcentre

Above: RAF BBMF Lancaster PA474 as Thumper Mk.III ready to taxy from outside the Flight's hangar at RAF Coningsby.
(Crown Copyright)

Below left: The Grand Slam bomb on show at the BBMF Visitor Centre, with volunteer guides Barry Woodhouse and Terry Hancock lending scale to the weapon.
(Author's Collection)

Below: Dambusters' exhibition in the BBMF Visitor Centre.
(Author's Collection)

During each season the flight is typically tasked to fly over 100 displays.

The Dam Busters film

Below: The dramatic advertising poster for director Michael Anderson's film The Dam Busters.

Below right: The wooden 'Y-shaped' 'coat-hanger' bombsight was not universally popular amongst the Dams Raid bomb aimers, as it could be difficult to hold steady with one hand. (all images on these pages courtesy of STUDIOCANAL Films Ltd)

The 1955, Associated British Picture Corporation, epic docu-drama The Dam Busters is one of the best-known and loved British war films. This legendary account of the Dambusters' exploits has commanded the public's affections for over half a century and the film, as much as the Dams Raid itself, ensured the iconic status of the Dambusters and the Lancaster in the British public's psyche. Eric Coates' masterful and marvellously rousing Dam Busters March, used in the film score, is equally famous and is immediately recognisable to most of us.

Many people's knowledge of the Dams Raid is founded on the content of the film, which is fairly accurate historically... but took 'a few liberties' with the facts. Part of the charm of the film is that it was made so soon after the war that the characters, the language and the atmosphere are very much of the era. However, this proximity to the actual events it portrays also meant that some aspects of the operation, and particularly of the Upkeep bouncing bomb, were still classified and not yet released into the public domain. As a result there had to be some guesswork on behalf of the film-makers.

The film was based on Guy Gibson's own account of the raid in his book Enemy Coast Ahead, which was published posthumously in 1946, and Paul Brickhill's bestseller The Dam Busters, which was first published in 1951. Australian journalist and author Paul Brickhill was himself a former RAF wartime fighter pilot (he flew Spitfires and Hurricanes with 74, 274 and 92 Squadrons) and he was also a prisoner of war in Stalag Luft III. As such, he brought an intimate knowledge of the behaviour and jargon of the RAF characters into his book, as well as an understanding of the flying details.

The screenplay for the film was written by the acclaimed British playwright R C Sherriff who, like Paul Brickhill, also had a military background – in his case as a captain in the British Army fighting in the trenches during the First World War. His understanding of the military system and of the fighting man informed his writing and made his screen adaption of the book all the more convincing. It is Sherriff's thoughtful and clear-sighted screenplay that is regarded by many as the magic ingredient that has made the film one of the most enduring war films of all time, not least because of the understated way in which the story is told.

The film was directed by Michael Anderson, who was relatively unknown at the time. Anderson decided to shoot the film in monochrome, although it could have been made in colour. This allowed original wartime footage to be seamlessly inserted and gave a gritty documentary style to the film that the use of colour would not have achieved.

Inevitably, there was some simplification of a complicated story that led to some aspects being left out of the film altogether. The film mentions only the Mohne, Eder and Sorpe dams as targets during the planning and briefing. It covers only the first wave attacks, ignoring the problems and losses suffered by

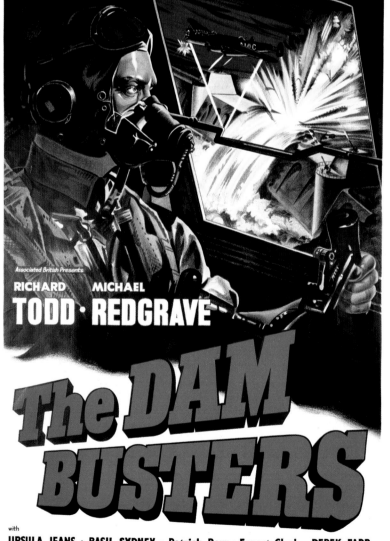

Associated British Presents

RICHARD MICHAEL
TODD · REDGRAVE

The DAM
BUSTERS

with
URSULA JEANS · BASIL SYDNEY · Patrick Barr · Ernest Clark · DEREK FARR
Screenplay by R. C. Sherriff · Directed by Michael Anderson · Distributed by Associated British-Pathe Ltd.

54.1
PROD. 64

the other two waves of the real raid, and it does not deal with the attacks on the Sorpe which were unsuccessful.

Artistic licence also caused some aspects of the story to be altered from the facts. Barnes Wallis was not actually the originator of the idea to attack the dams as the film suggests; the dams had already been identified as an important target by the Air Ministry before the war started. Neither was it as single-handed a campaign against bureaucracy for Wallis as the film makes out and he did not encounter the level of total opposition which is portrayed. In the film, the idea of the 'spotlights altimeter' for setting the aircraft's height accurately at 60ft over water was credited to Gibson after he had seen spotlights in action at a show in London, but this did not actually happen and it was Benjamin Lockspeiser, the director of scientific research at the Ministry of Aircraft Production, who devised the concept. The wooden Y-shaped 'coat hanger' bomb sight intended to enable crews to release the weapon at the right distance from the target, which is given prominence in the film, was not wholly successful; some bomb aimers used it, but others came up with their own solutions, such as pieces of string in the bomb-aimer's position and markings on the acrylic glass blister.

One of the most obvious deviations from fact was that the mock-up Upkeep bombs carried by the Lancasters in the film were spherical rather than the true cylindrical shape. They were also slightly larger and deeper than the real weapon, accentuating the overall shape for the benefit of the cameras. The full details of Upkeep were not declassified until 1963 and so were not available to the film makers, and the actual test footage was censored to hide any details of the test bombs. Somewhat amusingly and fairly typically, Barnes Wallis tried to explain the theory of the bomb to the film's director, Michael Anderson, but then suddenly realised that it was still on the secret list. "Oh dear, I can't possibly tell you any more," he exclaimed, "I've probably said too much already." The relatively minor deviations from fact do not make the film any less enjoyable, but could cause some to misunderstand the full details and realities of the original operation.

The two lead parts were played by the brilliantly well cast Richard Todd, who played Gibson, and Michael Redgrave, who played Wallis. Todd bore a remarkably close physical resemblance to Gibson. He also had a military wartime background as an Army captain in the infantry and later with the Parachute Regiment, being parachuted into Normandy in the early hours of D-Day. Like many of the other actors with military service behind them, he had a military bearing, he knew how to salute, he felt comfortable and at home

Above: Richard Todd as Gibson and Michael Redgrave as Wallis celebrate a successful first trial of Upkeep. Probably filmed at Gibraltar Point near Skegness, Lincolnshire.

Barnes Wallis tried to explain the theory of the bomb to the director, but then realised that it was still on the secret list.

Filming one of the Lancasters taxying at Hemswell. The strange shape of the mock-up Upkeep is apparent and the twin 0.50in guns in the rear turret are also factually inaccurate.

in uniform and knew how the military rank structure operated. Michael Redgrave also bore a likeness to the real Wallis; he was, of course, a brilliant actor, he spent time with Wallis and this allowed him to give a highly realistic portrayal of the character of the real Wallis on screen.

Some of the other actors who played the parts of the various aircrew or senior officers had also served in the Forces during the Second World War. One example being Nigel Stock who played Pilot Officer 'Spam' Spafford, Gibson's navigator; he had fought with the Army in Burma, twice being mentioned in dispatches and ending the war as a major. Most of the filming took place at the RAF stations of Scampton and Hemswell (with Hemswell being used for the majority of ground filming and for most of the airfield flying scenes). Inevitably, there was some confusion among the service personnel at the RAF bases used for the filming, as to who was who, and some young airmen saluted the actors who looked the part of the officers they were playing. Eventually orders were issued for the actors to wear an armband when not filming to show that they were with the film unit.

Gibson's black Labrador dog was played by an Army mine-detector, explosive-sniffing dog, which very much looked the part and actually shared the original dog's name. Richard Todd was a dog-lover and, recognising the need to bond with the animal for the film, he persuaded the Army to let him take the animal on from its handler for the duration of the filming. The dog became his pet, staying with him in the White Hart Hotel in Lincoln when 'off duty'. It clearly worked, as the bond between man and dog is evident in the film and would be difficult to fabricate. When the dog eventually went back to his Army duties they had been together for three months.

For many, the biggest stars of the film are the Lancaster aircraft. When filming commenced in April 1954, only about nine years after the war had ended, Lancasters were already in short supply. The last RAF unit operating the Lancaster at this time was the School of Maritime Reconnaissance at St Mawgan, in Cornwall. The aircraft used in the film were four of the final production Lancaster Mk. B VIIs – NX673, NX679, NX782 and RT686 – which had to be taken out of storage at 20 Maintenance Unit, Aston Down in Gloucestershire. They were leased from the Air

There was some confusion and airmen saluted the actors who looked the part of officers they were playing.

Ministry, which charged for them on the basis of engine running hours (per engine). The cost was in the region of £7000 per Lancaster flying hour at today's equivalent prices.

Three of the aircraft (NX673, NX679 and RT686) were modified by a working party, from the A V Roe Repair Organisation at Bracebridge Heath near Lincoln, to resemble the Type 464 (Provisioning) Lancasters which flew on the Dams Raid. The mid-upper gun turrets were removed, along with the H2S radomes under the fuselage and the bomb bay doors. The bomb bays were further modified to create the authentic Dambusters look and the mock-up Upkeeps, made out of plywood and plaster of Paris, were suspended beneath them. One obvious difference with the Mk.VII Lancasters from the original versions was that these later Lancs had the Frazer-Nash FN82 rear turret with twin 0.50 inch machine guns, rather than the FN20 turret with four 0.303 inch machine guns, which were standard in 1943.

The existing white upper surfaces of the Lancasters, which had last served in the Far East, were over-painted rather hurriedly with the camouflage colours and pattern of the wartime bombers, and the 1950s underwing aircraft serial numbers were painted out. The aircraft wore different code letters on either side of the fuselage, enabling three aircraft to play the part of six on film. NX679 was painted to represent Gibson's ED932 AJ-G and it was the only aircraft to have its serial numbers altered for the film. One of the aircraft, NX782, was retained as a standard Lancaster coded ZN-G to represent Gibson's aircraft when he commanded 106 Squadron and was also used for the training flight sequences.

The Lancasters were operated from RAF Hemswell and some of the airfield scenes were filmed there. Some of the flying activity was filmed at RAF Kirton-in-Lindsey, which was still a grass airfield with no hard runways and therefore more closely resembled Scampton as it was at the time of the Dams Raid in May 1943. Four operational Avro Lincoln flight crews from 83 and 97 Squadrons at Hemswell were picked to fly the Lancasters for the film. Flight Lieutenant Ken Souter, a flight commander on 83 Squadron, led the crews for the filming; the other pilots were Flying Officer Dick Lambert and Polish pilots Flight Sergeant Joe Kmiecik AFM and Flight Sergeant Ted Szuwalski. All except Lambert had wartime operational flying experience. None had flown the Lancaster before, but there were many common features between the Lancaster and the Lincoln (the latter being a development of the former) and they were easily able to convert and were quickly conducting familiarisation flights, which were soon followed by low flying and close formation sorties for the cameras.

On the real raid, the Lancaster crews were required to be flown at 60ft on their attack runs. When this was recreated for the film in 1954, 60ft looked higher than it actually was and Erwin Hillier, the German-born director of photography and aerial photography, asked Ken and his pilots to fly lower, at 40ft. Despite the obvious risks, this is the height that much of the flying was conducted at for the filming; it was exhilarating for the pilots to be authorised to do this legally. The RAF pilots who flew the Lancasters are the unsung stars of the film; at the time they were not named and did not receive any credits, but Richard Todd said of them: "Those RAF

chaps in the film took a lot of chances and did a wonderful, wonderful job for us."

Flying scenes showing the early bouncing bomb tests were shot off the shoreline near Skegness in Lincolnshire, close to the main filming locations. The practice flights before the raid and the actual bombing runs over the dams were filmed along Lake Windermere and through the Kirkstone Pass in the Lake District, and at the Derwent reservoir and dam in the Derbyshire Peak District. Crossing the enemy coast was shot over Gibraltar Point near Skegness and near Southwold in Suffolk, and the flight over Holland to the dams was simulated over the flat fenlands of southern Lincolnshire and into Norfolk.

For the film, Richard Todd, as Gibson, and his flight engineer Sergeant Pulford, played by Robert Shaw, had to be seen starting up and taxying a Lancaster. They learned the complicated start-up sequence to perfection and carried out the procedure themselves, with an RAF flight engineer supervising them from out of sight on the cockpit floor. The start-up and taxying scenes were all shot at Hemswell and on one occasion Todd actually piloted a Lancaster on a take-off run up to 70mph, at which point he had to throttle back the engines and roll to a halt. Many of the in-cockpit shots were filmed at Elstree Studios in a specially built mock-up Lancaster cockpit, which was a sort of simple flight simulator as the controls were linked to

Above: Richard Todd, as Gibson, with the Army mine-detecting dog, which had the same name as Gibson's dog. Todd kept the dog as a pet for the duration of the filming.
(all images on these pages courtesy of STUDIOCANAL Films Ltd)

On the raid the Lancasters were flown at 60ft... the director of photography asked the pilots to fly lower, at 40ft.

Above: Storyboard showing a variety of scenes from The Dam Busters film. (image courtesy of STUDIOCANAL Films Ltd)

a motor beneath the platform and created the appropriate movement. It was here, in the many waiting moments between takes, that Todd was taught to fly the platform correctly by an RAF pilot.

Once filming was completed, the four Lancasters that had helped to recreate the epic Dambusters story were returned from whence they came, 20 MU at Aston Down, without fuss or ceremony. They languished there until they were declared surplus to requirements and were then unceremoniously cut up and sold to a scrap metal company in July 1956.

The film had its world premiere at the Empire cinema in London's Leicester Square on May 16, 1955 (the 12th anniversary of the Dams Raid). Demand for tickets was so great that two Royal Command performances were held on the same night. Some of the surviving aircrew from the Dams Raid attended the first showing.

The four Lancasters that helped recreate the epic story were declared surplus to requirements and then cut up.

With its very British stiff upper lip depiction, the film manages to paint a picture of the RAF men for whom the extremes of aerial warfare were just a job; flyers for whom hazardous missions, anti-aircraft fire and the prospect, every time they took off, that this mission could be their last, were quite simply the accepted facets of many a night's work. The Dam Busters film is refreshingly free of heroics while remaining, indubitably, a film about heroes.

THE DAM BUSTERS MOVIE REMAKE

New Zealand film maker Sir Peter Jackson, well known for his Lord of the Rings and Hobbit films, has been planning to produce a remake of The Dam Busters since 2006. His last Hobbit film, The Hobbit: The Battle of Five Armies, was released in 2014 and since then he has worked on another fantasy film called Mortal Engines and a second Tintin movie, while the Dambusters film has been put on hold. The new movie, if it is ever made, will be produced by Jackson's Wingnut company and was originally slated to be the directorial debut of visual effects specialist Christian Rivers, but Rivers' debut is now set to be Mortal Engines. The Dambusters screenplay was completed some years ago by writer and actor Stephen Fry, and a number of highly realistic full-scale models of Lancaster bombers were built but have been in long-term storage for perhaps a decade.

However, it seems Jackson has not forgotten about the Dambusters, and remains keenly aware of public interest in a remake of the classic film. Back in 2015, he said: "There is only a limited span I can abide, of people driving me nuts asking me when I'm going to do that project. So I'll have to do it. I want to, actually, it's one of the truly great true stories of the Second World War, a wonderful, wonderful story."

It appears the Dambusters remake will eventually happen. It has a hard act to follow.

Lancaster over the
Derwent

What is it actually like to fly a 30 ton Second World War heavy bomber at very low level among the hills, over water and across a dam? One modern day pilot who has had the rare privilege of experiencing just that is Squadron Leader Stuart Reid BSc RAF (Retired). For 11 years, between 1999 and 2010, Stuart flew Avro Lancaster PA474 with the RAF Battle of Britain Memorial Flight (RAF BBMF), and in 2008 he flew the RAF BBMF Lancaster on commemorative flypasts over Howden, Derwent and Ladybower reservoirs.

Here he describes the background to the events and provides a pilot's perspective of the experience of flying a 'Lanc' in these circumstances; he also gives his opinion of the difficulties which faced the Dambuster pilots doing it for real in 1943:

Of all the events that the RAF BBMF aircraft and flight crews participate in, commemorations of celebrated major Allied operations that took place during the Second World War are among the most important and poignant. One such event that I had the very good fortune to participate in on May 16, 2008, was that of the 65th anniversary of Operation Chastise, the 617 Squadron attack on the dams in Germany.

The plan for the commemorative flypast was to take Lancaster PA474 over the Peak District to fly down the Howden reservoir, along Derwent reservoir and over the Derwent dam, and then over Ladybower reservoir to re-enact the training sorties flown by the 617 Squadron crews in preparation for the Dams Raid. Derwent dam was one of the practice targets in April and May 1943, and its position deep in the hills to the north of the Hope valley presented the crews with one of the most challenging of simulated attacks.

The 65th anniversary commemoration ceremony was to be held at the Derwent dam in the presence of Dambuster veterans, including Squadron Leader Les Munro CNZM DSO QSO DFC. The flypast routine was to consist of PA474 performing three passes over the Derwent dam, followed by a short, circuitous route to reposition for a further flypast over the dam concurrent with a flypast by two Tornado GR4 aircraft from the present 617 Squadron. The minimum

By Squadron Leader Stuart Reid BSc RAF (Retired)

Above: The enormity of the original raid is revealed when viewing the aircraft and the Derwent dam, as Lancaster PA474 is dwarfed by the structure.
(Crown Copyright)

Being a priceless artefact of the nation's aviation heritage, high airspeeds, high pitch rates and rapid roll rates are avoided and are usually unnecessary.

authorised height for PA474 over the reservoirs above the Derwent and the dam itself was 100ft.

The ceremony was to be televised. There would be live coverage of the flypasts from ground based cameras at the Derwent dam and from helicopters that would hover high over Ladybower reservoir to film the Lancaster as it made its way down the upper Derwent Valley from Howden reservoir. Planning for the sortie was uncomplicated; the forecast weather was overcast but generally good enough for the flypast, although there was the possibility of low cloud over the high fells of the central Peak District. The final sortie brief was completed in company with the TV helicopter crews to finalise all timings and to ensure that all flypast choreography was understood by the participating crews and the TV camera team.

The TV helicopter crews were known to the BBMF. They had been at Coningsby the previous year to provide coverage of the first flight of PA474, in its guise as Phantom of the Ruhr, following its official unveiling after six months of maintenance carried out by Air Atlantique at Coventry. This familiarity did not get in the way of ensuring that everyone understood the positioning of all aircraft with respect to one another so as not to present a hazard. The briefing was the last opportunity to ensure this.

As with most of the major ceremonial events involving the RAF BBMF aircraft, a large crowd of enthusiastic well-wishers had gathered at the boundary fence adjacent to the west end of the flight's hangar. The start-up, taxi-out and engine power checks were completed in good time to minimise the risk of a delay caused by minor aircraft serviceability issues. The BBMF C-47 Dakota ZA947 departed ahead of us to position on route ahead of PA474 for the air-to air photoshoot with the ITN camera team on board. After take-off, I rendezvoused with the 'Dak' and positioned PA474 in close formation on the left side for the news camera team to film from the open parachute door on ZA947. After the photoshoot was complete, we continued north-west to the Peak

District to refine the timing for the first flypast.

Fortunately, the cloud had lifted off the hill tops as we climbed over the fells and approached the area to the north of Howden reservoir. I flew the aircraft on a heading perpendicular to the initial inbound track to the reservoir, so as to refine the timing as accurately as possible for the first flypast over the dam. Looking to my left I could see the reservoirs in the Derwent valley stretching away to the south and with the timing now spot-on I turned the bomber to the left to set up for the steep descent on to Howden reservoir.

The upper reaches of Howden reservoir are set into steep sided, wood covered valleys and required me to manoeuvre PA474 with some dexterity to achieve the rate of descent needed to achieve the optimum flight path over the reservoir, while maintaining safe separation from the valley sides and without subjecting the aircraft to undue stress. The initial manoeuvre called for about 45 degrees of bank to the left, together with the application of back-pressure on the controls to prevent the nose from dropping too low during the turn. In the Lancaster it is extremely hazardous if the aircraft's nose is allowed to drop too low while rolling or banked at low-level.

I have always been conscious of the need for considerate handling of PA474. Although operating at relatively light all-up weights in comparison to the Lancasters flown by the wartime crews, the aircraft is, nonetheless, always flown with fatigue conservation in mind. Being a priceless artefact of the nation's aviation heritage, high airspeeds, high pitch rates and rapid roll rates are avoided and are usually unnecessary unless safety of flight dictates otherwise.

Despite having the capability to inflict immense destructive power in war, at peace PA474 is a wonderful, graceful 'Old Lady' of the skies and it is my opinion that it should always be handled with the dignity and respect befitting such a cherished 'Elder Statesperson' of the historic aircraft community.

With 1900rpm set, the throttles were brought back to minus four (inches boost) to maintain the airspeed at around 150 Knots Indicated Air Speed (KIAS) in the initial descent into the upper valley. I immediately became aware of the proximity of the aircraft to the valley sides and I was working quite hard to keep the bomber descending safely within the confines of the valley and out on to Howden reservoir. I needed both hands on the control yoke, combined with judicious use of rudder to coax the aircraft onto the desired flight path and, as I coerced the Lanc about the sky, I very much appreciated the strength and security the seat provided. The pilot's seat of the Lancaster is one heck of a piece of engineering.

Once clear of the steep valley sides and over the water, the throttles were opened slightly to minus two to maintain the airspeed in what was to be a continuous gradual descent to the Derwent reservoir further down the valley. I S-turned the aircraft to ease around the shoreline taking the optimum racing line towards the centre of the dam at the southern end of Howden reservoir. Approaching Howden reservoir dam in a gentle descending right turn, I became aware of a cluster of trees protruding above the level of the dam wall from what appeared to be a small island or promontory immediately beyond the left far side of the dam as I looked at it. I eased the rate of descent momentarily and manoeuvred PA474 to the right of the trees to cross the dam on to Derwent reservoir and, once clear of the trees, continued the descent to achieve 100ft Minimum Separation Distance (MSD) above the surface of Derwent reservoir. With the aircraft now level, the airspeed was reduced to about 145KIAS and zero boost set in preparation for opening the bomb doors. The bomb bay of Lancaster PA474 differs from the Dambuster Type 464 aircraft in having the bomb doors attached, so I thought opening the bomb doors would add to the spectacle of the first flypast over the dam.

At this stage, the Derwent dam was unsighted to me, being screened by the valley sides in which we were flying. However, as I again eased PA474 around another racing line to follow the valley first to the left, then to the right to align with what I thought be the ideal attack track, the dam became visible about a mile ahead. It was at this stage I realised how little time the 617 Squadron crews had to stabilise their aircraft on the very precise Upkeep release parameters needed to stand any chance of success as they committed to their attacks, especially by night and when they were likely to be under heavy enemy anti-aircraft fire. I manoeuvred PA474 to achieve the best position for the flypast over the dam and, with the alignment set, called for the bomb doors to be opened and for 2400rpm to make the engines sing a bit for the benefit of the spectators below – you've heard of The Three Tenors, well I present The Four Merlins. To me they sound just as good. The Lancaster stirs the soul at the best of times, but it is always a very special moment to savour, as 'Merlin Song' resounds through the aircraft, while at the controls of one of the most iconic aircraft to have graced the skies in honour of one of the most famous events in military history.

It was one of those unique, once in a lifetime, never to be repeated experiences and very emotive to overfly the dam in honour of the 617 Squadron crews and to think that the aircraft looked and sounded just as it did over 65 years previously – it really was soul stirring stuff.

I completed the two further passes before commencing the short navigation route to reposition for the final flypast to coincide with the 617 Squadron Tornado GR4s. Now, with more time to take in the landscape around us, what became apparent was the large number of parked vehicles on the roads above the Derwent reservoir. My eyes were then drawn to the clusters of onlookers gathered on the hillsides above the Derwent Valley. It was clear the event was of great interest to many enthusiasts who had made their way into the hills to see and, of greater significance, hear the symbolic spectacle of a Lancaster once again over the Derwent dam. Following the final flypast, I flew PA474 down the Derwent Valley past Chatsworth House to clear the area before returning to RAF Coningsby.

On the return flight to RAF Coningsby, I had time to reflect and realised that I had been in an extremely privileged position. I had seen the Derwent dam almost as the 617 crews had seen it, heard the power of the Merlins almost as they had heard them and flown the aircraft almost exactly as they had flown it decades before. From my perspective as a pilot, it didn't get any better than that. I had also obtained a unique insight into the significance of what the 617 Squadron crews achieved. During the turning descent into the valley above the upper reaches of the Howden reservoir, I became very conscious of the huge difficulties facing the crews in training for their wartime mission. I was flying a relatively lightweight Lancaster by day, with the benefit of some 30 years flying experience as an RAF pilot, many of which had been at the controls of high performance bomber aircraft, equipped with state of the art navigation and weapon aiming systems. It made me realise how primitive the technology available to the 617 crews had been by modern standards, and it gave me a far greater appreciation of the immeasurable demands placed on the crews to succeed with their gruelling mission.

The 21st century RAF utilises equipment designed to fulfil a specific purpose, which has undergone many years of painstaking research and development before being put into service. However, in 1943 the 617 Squadron crews were at the forefront of everything they were doing. The Lancaster, one of the first four-engine bombers, had flown for the first time barely two years before and the ingenious Upkeep weapon system was still under development by Barnes Wallis as the crews were in training. To add to the challenge, the crews were employing untried tactics and arduous navigational techniques that would be put to the test for the first time against three foreboding targets, deep in enemy territory, with a unique weapon that they would be dropping live for the first time during the attack.

The whole venture is unthinkable by modern standards, having evolved from a concept to a spectacular success in a matter of weeks, yet Barnes Wallis and the 617 Squadron crews managed to pull it off. I doubt a similar endeavour could be undertaken today in such timescales, it was a truly remarkable achievement. I remember talking to a B-17 pilot about the relative merits of the two bombers (Lancaster and B-17) and how, while the B-17 was a fine bomber that had served with great success and distinction, for some reason it didn't quite capture the imagination in the same way as the Lancaster. His response was that it was because the B-17 didn't have its Dambusters equivalent to give the Flying Fortress equal prominence in history to the Lancaster. If ever there was a statement to highlight the significance to RAF, military and world history of the contribution made by 617 Squadron, Barnes Wallis and the Avro Lancaster, that was it.

'Apres moi le deluge'.

Above: Lancaster PA474 banks hard over Howden Reservoir, descending into the steep-sided wooded valley. (Crown Copyright)

An RAF F-35B is flown by Squadron Leader Hugh Nichols just off the south coast of England on July 1, 2016.

A squadron REBORN

Having flown Tornados since 1983, 617 Squadron was disbanded in 2014 and re-formed in 2017 to fly Britain's latest all-weather multirole fighter – the Lockheed Martin F-35B Lightning II.

After several years of testing and training in the US, including the type's first ski-jump launch in 2015, the RAF has been making preparations for the unit to take up residence at RAF Marham, Norfolk.

The UK's F-35 fleet is set to operate off the new HMS *Queen Elizabeth* and HMS *Prince of Wales* aircraft carriers and as of February 2018, 14 of the 18 F-35Bs bought so far had been delivered.

The Ministry of Defence has said it ultimately intends to buy a total of 138 F-35s, although some of these future purchases are likely to be F-35As, which have greater range but lack the short take-off and landing capability of the F-35B. Three of the UK's F-35s will remain in the US at Edwards Air Force Base for testing and evaluation purposes.

617 Squadron commanding officer Wing Commander John Butcher said that the original Dambusters crews would have been "quite amazed" by the F-35B's capabilities.

He said that the aircraft would "really chime with them. And for me, I can see a lot of parallels with what we are being asked to do now. We are bringing very special technology into service – one again for a very, very special mission,

which is to bring stealth and combat air capability to UK defence. I think there is a nice link there between what our forefathers did with 617 Squadron and what we are doing now."

Shortly after first taking the controls of an F-35, Wg Cdr Butcher he said: "It was a real thrill finally to fly this aircraft and it certainly exceeded my expectations. The capabilities and potential of this aircraft are immense and this is a very exciting time to be a fast jet pilot."

During the course of his career, Wg Cdr Butcher has flown Harriers from HMS *Illustrious* and F/A-18 Hornets off the decks of two US Navy aircraft carriers, and said he was looking forward to making his first landing on the deck of HMS *Queen Elizabeth*: "It will be fantastic to then add a third aircraft to another class of aircraft carrier and an absolute privilege to do that and to lead 617 Squadron as it takes on that new venture."

A new £92 million F-35 flight simulator was due to arrive at RAF Marham during the summer of 2018 and it was hoped that the new jet would achieve initial operating capability (IOC) in the land-based role by December 2018. The first flight trials off HMS *Queen Elizabeth* were also scheduled to take place towards the end of 2018 with IOC for carrier-based operations due by December 2020.

It seems as though the story of the Dambusters unit, 617 Squadron, is far from over.

Below left: An F-35B flies over RAF Marham, the new home of 617 Squadron – the Dambusters.

Below centre: The first of the UK's F-35Bs, pictured here performing at the Royal International Air Tattoo 2016 at RAF Fairford.

Below right: RAF and Royal Navy personnel were at Eglin Air Force Base, Florida, USA, to familiarise themselves with F-35 air and ground procedures. Pictured is an RAF F-35B at Eglin.